House of Gold

Maria Bambina –
Morning Star, Mystical Rose

A Marian Consecration to the Immaculate
and Sorrowful Infant Heart of Mary

Mary Elizabeth Anne Kloska, Fiat.+

En Route Books and Media, LLC
Saint Louis, MO, USA

✇ENROUTE
Make the time

En Route Books and Media, LLC
5705 Rhodes Avenue
St. Louis, MO 63109

Illustrations by Mary Kloska

Copyright © 2022 Mary Kloska

ISBN-13 978-1-956715-56-9
Library of Congress Control Number available at
https://catalog.loc.gov/

Dedication –May 31, 2022
Feast of Our Lady's Visitation

I am so happy to have finished this book for May 31st, the Feast of Our Lady's Visitation. Having the name Mary Elizabeth, after the two holy women who we celebrate today, I always took the Feast of the Visitation as my special Feast Day. Our Lady has spent my entire lifetime blessing me with Her friendship –and so I rejoice today to offer Her this little gift of a book, which I hope brings many more souls into Her humble, Motherly embrace. When I was in kindergarten I was asked to write a small essay (three sentences) about who was my hero. I wrote: '*My hero is Mary (the Blessed Mother.)*' And I said something like '*I am named for Her and want to be like Her when I grow up.*' To be like Mary means to love like Mary –and that path of love at times contains thorns where we join Her in crucified Love with Her Son. But it also contains a great shower of grace (which She as our Mother wins for us by Her Immaculate Heart's prayer on our behalf.) How Providential that so many years later I am writing a book of Consecration to the Infant Immaculate and Sorrowful Heart of Mary –I, who wanted to 'be

i

like Her' when I grew up am asking Her as an adult to make me like She was as a small Child. I still look to the Blessed Mother as my Morning Star of Hope, the Star of the stormy Seas of this life. I turn to Her as the Mystic Rose –hidden, yet emanating Her powerful perfume of holiness everywhere She turns. I trust in Her as my Seat of Wisdom, teaching the best path to continually follow Her guidance towards heaven. She is my strong Tower of Ivory, sharing Her faithful courage with me in times of struggle. She is my House of Gold –radiating the Divine Presence of Her Son and constantly inviting me to enter *into Her Heart* to live in union with Him there. I consecrate this book to Her Motherly love as I offer it as a gift to the world –hoping and trusting that the Holy Spirit will use it to form many more little souls to be humble, pure and holy as She was, even from the first moment of Her Immaculate Conception.

And I offer this book to Jesus as well, in thanksgiving for the gift He gave to us under the Cross of such a Perfect Mother.

Sacred Heart of Jesus, we thank you!

Mary, my Mother, pray for us!

Mary Elizabeth Kloska, Fiat.

Table of Contents

Introduction
'Maria Bambina'

He took some dirt into His hands
He molded you for His Son, the Man
He placed you in the womb of Anne
Who prayed and begged for God's great plan
He smiled and whispered, 'This is good.'
You came forth from His Own Word.
La la la la la la Amen... Maria

Sweet Lullaby of your heartbeat
The pitter patter of your tiny feet
Within He placed emboldened faith
Bold humility –the strongest grace
The mystic fragrance of your breath
A love so fierce you feared no death
La la la la la la Amen... Maria

Little Mary, sweetest Child
Ever Virgin –so meek and mild
Innocence and morning Light
Fiery Way guiding us through night
Mystic Rose –Morning Star
Sleeping gently waiting for your call
La la la la la la Amen... Maria

Lily, Violet, smiling Sun
Wellspring of the holy One
Waterfall, Wisdom of fire
Hallelujah in the angel's choir
Little Dewdrop to quench His thirst
The Lord, your God, was always first
La la la la la la Amen... Maria

Mary, will you sing for me?
Praying Fiat to set us free
Perfect Lady, tender Heart
Praising heaven in Magnificat
God proposed... you agreed
And waited God's own Spirit's seed

Small Bambina, Heart so pure
Mother of our holy Lord
Can you teach me how to sing
Your hymn of love eternally?
Thank you, Mary, for saying 'yes'
All ages forth now call you blessed.
La la la la la la Amen... Maria
La la la la la la Amen... Bambina[1]

---

[1] Song 'Maria Bambina' written by Mary Kloska

St Francis de Sales on the Maria Bambina:

> *"Come close to Her cradle, think of the virtues of this holy infant. Question the angels, the cherubim and seraphim, ask them if they are equal in perfection to this little girl, and they will tell you that She infinitely surpasses them. See them surround Her cradle. Then as they regard Her a little more closely, ravished and beside themselves, they proceed in their admiration: Who is this that comes forth like the dawn, as beautiful as the moon, as resplendent as the sun, as awe-inspiring as bannered troops?"*

The Infant Mary's Heart is a great mystery of splendid grace. Every virtue was present in full from the first moments of Her Immaculate Conception. Unstained by the smallest of sins –Her Heart was a perfect Tabernacle for God from the first moment it began to beat –and for this reason this little Maria Bambina already bears the title 'House of Gold'. Being resplendent in divine love, holiness and beauty, little Mary was already the Morning Star whose presence on earth pointed towards the coming of the Savior. She was the Mystic Rose even as a little embryo in Her mother's womb. The word 'mystic' means 'hidden'. Our Lady has been hidden in God from the beginning –His Masterpiece of creation, the ideal archetype of woman from all eternity. She is called a Rose because it is the most beautiful of flowers. Mary is the perfect flower hidden in God. Each petal of Her Heart is a virtue lived in perfection, shedding both perfume and light on the world. These petals must be pure (Immaculate) and crushed (Sorrowful) to give their fragrance.

But in doing so, light comes from each petal as a point of a Star – for this reason Our Lady is also called the 'Morning Star' or 'Star of the Sea.'

St. Cardinal John Henry Newman says that Mary is called by two names that convey Her beauty: Mystical Rose and Morning Star. Our Lady is the most beautiful flower that ever was seen in the spiritual world. It is by the power of God's grace that from this barren and desolate earth there have ever sprung up at all flowers of holiness and glory. And Mary is the Queen of them. She is the Queen of spiritual flowers; and therefore She is called the *Rose*, for the rose is fitly called of all flowers the most beautiful. But Cardinal Newman says that it is the title 'Morning Star' which suits Her best because a rose belongs to the earth and has a short life. A star, instead, is high in heaven and abides forever. He writes, it is **"Mary's prerogative to be the *Morning* Star, which heralds in the sun. She does not shine for Herself, or from Herself, but She is the reflection of Her and our Redeemer, and She glorifies Him."**

We as children of Mary must be engrafted onto Her Heart and grow from the same source of Love as She has (which is the Divine Love of the Trinity indwelling within Her). United with Her as children within the womb of their Mother, we will grow to be little mystical rosebuds like Her, stars shining the Light of Christ in the tempests of this dark world, and little houses of gold, tabernacles of Divine Grace and Love in this world.

Mary is the "Domus Aurea," the House of Gold

'The Queen stands at His Right Hand arrayed in Gold!' (Ps 45:9)

Saint John Henry Newman explains the beautiful name *House of Gold* that Christian tradition has given to the Mother of God. She is compared to gold because it is the most beautiful, the most valuable and precious of all metals. Silver, copper, and steel have worth, but nothing is so rich, so splendid, as gold. For this reason in Scripture the Holy City is called Golden. St. John writes that *"The City was pure gold, as it were transparent glass."* This is written to give us an idea of the wondrous beautifulness of heaven, by comparing it with what is the most beautiful of all the substances which we see on earth.

Cardinal Newman says that *"therefore it is that Mary too is called golden; because Her graces, Her virtues, Her innocence, Her purity, are of that transcendent brilliancy and dazzling perfection."* Mary's holiness is of such transcendent brilliancy and dazzling perfection, so costly, so exquisite, that the angels cannot, so to say, keep their eyes off Her any more than we could help gazing upon any great work of gold. But She is more than this; She is a *House of Gold or Golden Palace* because *"She is the house and the palace of the Great King, of God Himself."* The Son of God once dwelt in this house. Jesus was born in this holy house; He took His flesh and blood from this house. Rightly then was She made to be of pure gold, because She was to give of that gold to form the body of the Son of God. She was golden in Her conception, golden in Her birth. She went through the fire of Her suffering like gold in the furnace, and when She ascended on high, Scripture says *'The Queen stands at His Right Hand arrayed in Gold!'* (Ps 45:9)

We, too, are children of Mary. When we allow Our Lady to conform ourselves to Christ, we, too, are made into a house of gold to be tabernacles for the living God. Just as Jesus is the Head – formed from the golden flesh and blood of Mary –so, too, we as His body are formed in Her, from Her. Just as Our Lady was a Tabernacle for Jesus, we are called to become a house of gold –a radiant monstrance of virtue –where He dwells and shines forth His Light on this world. My prayer is that as we meditate on Our Lady under the title House of God, Mystic Rose, Morning Star of the Sea that we will come to imitate Her virtues and that by making a consecration to Her Little Heart under these titles that we, too, will shine as houses of gold for the Lord.

CHAPTER 1
History of Devotion to the Maria Bambina
(Infant Mary)

(The following excerpt is taken from Chapter 3 of Mary Kloska's book '*Raising Children of the Cross*'.) :

Besides Jesus, there has never been a more perfect Child than the Infant Mary. She was immaculately conceived, which means that Her Heart was so unstained by sin (both original and actual sin) that from the first moments of Her existence, Her Heart was a garden castle where the Holy Trinity could dwell in full.

We adore Jesus in His Divine Childhood. In the same way, we venerate Mary in her childhood. Mary is the Woman chosen by God at the beginning of time in Genesis (Genesis 3:15) to bring forth the Savior –and to do that She was immaculately conceived. This means that God took the merits of Christ's Passion and went back in time and applied them to Our Lady when She was conceived. The redemption of Jesus was applied earlier in time because He is eternal and outside of time. By doing this, God was creating a perfect Tabernacle (the first home –being that of Our Mother's womb) for His Divine Son. This means that Our Lady was Immaculate –perfect –and that Her Infant Heart never changed throughout Her life (like ours becomes stained through sin and needs Confession and the Sacraments to renew it). Mary's Immaculate Heart is the same at Her birth as it was under Calvary. Mary's Heart pierced with swords under the cross was an Infant Heart –total in Her innocence and purity pierced with pain. Purity is the presence of God –and Our Lady called *'full of grace'* by the angel Gabriel when He visited Her at the Annunciation was most pure and most humble, therefore making Her so full of the presence of God.

This perfect Heart of the Child Mary is foreshadowed by the Book of Wisdom 7: 22-30:

> *"For in her is a spirit intelligent, holy, unique, manifold, subtle, agile, clear, unstained, certain, never harmful, loving the good, keen, unhampered, beneficent, kindly, firm, secure, tranquil, all-powerful, allseeing, and pervading all spirits, though they be intel-*

ligent, pure and very subtle. For Wisdom is mobile beyond all motion, and she penetrates and pervades all things by reason of her purity. For she is a breath of the might of God and a pure emanation of the glory of the Almighty; therefore nothing defiled can enter into her. For she is the reflection of eternal light, the spotless mirror of the power of God, the image of his goodness. Although she is one, she can do all things, and she renews everything while herself purduring; Passing into holy souls from age to age, she produces friends of God and prophets. For God loves nothing so much as the one who dwells with Wisdom. For she is fairer than the sun and surpasses every constellation of the stars. Compared to light, she is found more radiant; though night supplants light, wickedness does not prevail over Wisdom."

For centuries, the Church has celebrated Mary's Nativity on September 8th – Hers being one of only three birthdays so honored, the other two being those of Jesus and His Precursor (St. John the Baptist). All three of these were born without the stain of original sin. St. John was filled with the Holy Spirit while in his mother's womb (Luke 1:13-17, 44) whereas Jesus and Mary were *conceived* full of grace.

The Feast of the Birth of Mary was first celebrated in the East by the Church of Jerusalem. In the fifth century a Byzantine church was erected there, on the spot where a tradition says the house of

Sts. Anne and Joachim once stood and became a focal point for her birthday celebration. Unfortunately, the original church was decimated during the Crusades. A new church was later built on that spot; this one still stands today and is a center of pilgrimage. The Catholic Church adopted this joyful feast by the seventh century by Pope Sergius I and the feast was celebrated every September 8th.

On the other hand, the Feast of the Most Holy Name of Mary commemorates the day the Blessed Virgin was named a few days after Her birth in accordance with the Jewish Law. The Feast was originated in Spain and was approved by the Holy See in 1513 then later extended to the whole Church by Pope Innocent XI in 1683 in thanksgiving to Our Lady for the Victory of John Sobleski, King of Poland, over the Turks, who were besieging Vienna and threatening the West. This Feast of the Holy Name of Mary is celebrated each year on September 12th.

The Feast of the Presentation of Mary that is celebrated every November 21st is also very ancient, going back to the sixth century in the Eastern Orthodox Church and it is one of the thirteen Great Feasts of the Church, often depicted in icons. The Catholic Church, however, did not adopt it until the fourteenth century.

Most of what we know of Our Lady's childhood is known through apocryphal sources and the writings of mystic saints like St. Bridget of Sweden, Blessed Anne Katherine Emmerich and Venerable Maria de Agreda, who were favored with the visions of Her childhood. From these works, we were able to have a glimpse of the early life of the Blessed Virigin Mary. We learn that her parents were St. Anne and St. Joachim (whose Feasts we celebrate on

July 26th), that She was born late in their life and dedicated to the Temple at an early age. Here we can read in St. Bridget's own words what Our Lady revealed to her about Her Childhood:

The Childhood, Life and Miracles of the Virgin Mary in Her own words revealed to St. Bridget:

"I am the Queen of Heaven. Love my Son, for he is most worthy; when you have him, you have all that is worthwhile. He is also most desirable; when you have him, you have all that is desirable. Love him, too, for he is most virtuous; when you have him, you have every virtue. I want to tell you how wonderful his love for my body and soul was and how much he honored my name. My Son loved me before I loved him, since he is my Creator.

He united my father and mother in a marriage so chaste that there could not be found a more chaste marriage at that time. They never wanted to come together except in accordance with the Law, and only then with the intention to bring forth offspring.

When an angel revealed to them that they would give birth to the Virgin from whom the salvation of the world would come, they would rather have died than to come together in carnal love; lust was dead in them. I assure you that when they did come together, it was because of divine love and because of the angel's message, not out of carnal desire, but against their will and out of a holy love for God. In this way, my flesh was put together by their seed and through divine love. Then, when my body had been made and formed, God infused the created soul into it from his divinity, and the soul was immediately sanctified along with the body, and the angels guarded and served it day and night. When my soul was sanctified and joined to its body, my mother felt such great joy that it would have been impossible to describe it!

Afterwards, when my lifetime had been accomplished, my Son first raised up my soul - for it was the mistress of the body - to a more excellent place than others in heaven, right next to his Divinity. Later, he also raised up my body in such a manner that no other creature's body is so close to God as mine. See how much my Son loved my soul and body! Yet, there are some people with a malevolent spirit who deny that I was assumed into Heaven, body and soul, and also others who simply do not know any better. But this is a most certain truth: I, with body and soul, was assumed to the Divinity!

Hear now how much my Son honored my name! My name is Mary, as it is said in the Gospel. When the angels hear this name, they rejoice in their mind and thank God for the great mercy that he worked through me and with me and because they see my Son's Humanity glorified in his Divinity. Those within the fire of purgatory rejoice exceedingly, just like a sick and bedridden man does if he receives a word of comfort that pleases his soul: he is suddenly overjoyed! When the good angels hear my name, they immediately move closer to the righteous for whom they are guardians, and rejoice over their progress in good deeds and virtues.

All humans have been given both good angels for their protection, and bad angels to test them. The good angels are not separated from God; they serve the soul without leaving God. They are constantly in his sight. Yet they work to inflame and incite the soul to do good. All the demons, however, shudder with fear at the name of Mary! When they hear the name, "Mary", they immediately release a soul out of the claws with which they had held her. Just as a bird or hawk, with its claws and beak embedded into its prey, releases it immediately if it hears a sound, but soon returns when it sees that no action follows, so do the demons - frightened when they hear my name – release the soul. But they return and fly back as fast as an arrow if no improvement follows.

No one is so cold in his love of God (unless he is damned) that he will not experience the devil releasing him from his habitual sins if only he invokes my name with the true intention of never returning to his evil deeds. The devil will never return to him unless he resumes the will to commit mortal sins. Sometimes, though, the devil is allowed to trouble him for the sake of his greater reward. However, the devil shall never own him.

"I am the Queen of Heaven, the Mother of God. I told you to wear a brooch on your chest. I will now show you

more fully how, from the beginning, when I first heard and understood that God existed, I always, and with fear, was concerned about my salvation and my observance of his commandments. But when I learned more about God - that he was my Creator and the judge of all my actions - I loved him more dearly, and I was constantly fearful and watchful so as to not offend him by word or deed.

Later, when I heard that he had given the Law and the commandments to the people and worked such great miracles through them, I made a firm decision in my soul to never love anything but him, and all worldly things became most bitter to me. When still later I heard that God himself would redeem the world and be born of a Virgin, I was seized by such great love for him that I thought of nothing but God and desired nothing but him. I withdrew myself, as much as I was able, from the conversation and presence of parents and friends, and I gave away all my possessions to the poor, and kept nothing for myself but meager food and clothing.

Nothing was pleasing to me but God! I always wished in my heart to live until the time of his birth, and perhaps, deserve to become the unworthy handmaid of the Mother of God. I also promised in my heart to keep my virginity, if this was acceptable to him, and to have no possessions in the world. However, if God wanted otherwise, my will was that his will, not mine, be done; for I believed that he could do all things and wanted nothing but what was beneficial and best for me. Therefore, I entrusted all my will to him.

When the time approached for the virgins to be presented in the temple of the Lord, I was also among them due to the devout compliance of my parents to the Law. I thought to myself that nothing was impossible for God, and since he knew that I wanted and desired nothing but him, I knew that he could protect my virginity, if it pleased him. However, if not, I wanted his will to be done. After I had heard all the commandments in the temple, I returned home, burning even more now than ever before with the love of God, being inflamed daily with new fires and desires of love.

For this reason, I withdrew myself even more from everyone, and was alone day and night, fearing greatly, and most of all, that my mouth should say anything, or my ears hear anything against the will of my God, or that my eyes see anything alluring or harmful. I was also afraid in the silence, and very worried that I might be silent about things of which I should, instead, have spoken.

While I was worried in my heart like this, alone by myself and placing all my hope in God, an inspiration about God's great power came over me, and I recalled how the angels and everything created serve him, and how his glory is indescribable and unlimited. While I was thus fascinated by this thought, I saw three wonderful things: I saw a star, but not the kind that shines in the sky; I saw a light, but not the kind that shines in this world; I smelled a fragrance, but not of herbs or anything else of this world. It was most delightful and truly indescribable, and it filled me up so completely that I jubilated with joy!

After this, I immediately heard a voice - but not from a human mouth - and when I heard it, I shuddered with the great fear that it might be an illusion, or a mockery by an evil spirit. But shortly after this, an angel of God appeared before me; he was like the most handsome of men, but not in the flesh as is the body of a created man, and he said to me: 'Hail, full of grace, the Lord is with thee!' When I heard this, I wondered what he meant and why he had come to me with such a greeting, for I knew and believed that I was unworthy of any such thing - or any good thing! However, I also knew that nothing is impossible for God, if he desires it.

Then the angel spoke again: 'The child to be born in you is holy and will be called the Son of God. May his will be done as it pleases him.' But, not even then did I consider myself worthy, and I did not ask the angel why, or when, this would happen. Instead I asked him how it could be that I, an unworthy maiden, who did not know any man, should become the Mother of God. The angel answered me (as I have just said): 'Nothing is impossible for God, for whatever he wants to do will be done.'

When I had heard these words of the angel, I felt the most fervent desire to become the Mother of God, and my soul spoke out of love and desire, saying: 'See, here I am; your will be done in me!' With these words, my Son was conceived in my womb to the indescribable joy of my soul and my every limb! While I had him in my womb, I bore him without any pain, without any heaviness or discomfort. I humbled myself in all things, knowing that he whom I bore was the Almighty!..."

The Maria Bambina in Milan, Italy

Devotion to the Infant Mary has also spread through pious devotion of the priests (Popes), religious and laity of the Church. As far back as 1007, the people of Milan, Italy built a church dedicated to the Maria Bambina. The church "Santa Maria Fulcorina" was dedicated to the "Mystery of the Nativity of Mary" and eventually became the cathedral church of Milan. The present-day cathedral was built, and was later consecrated by St. Charles Borromeo in A.D. 1572 and dedicated to "Mariae Nascenti" -- "The Nativity of Mary." This city, then, became one of the centers of devotion to the Child Mary. In 1251, the Pope granted special indulgences to anyone who visited that church on September 8th, the feast of Her birthday.

The devotion to the Infant Mary spread even further in Italy, when in 1735 a religious sister made a wax image of Our Lady as a baby –this statue traveled around to several locations and in 1884 ended up in a convent of sisters. The statue had faded to grey, but while in the custody of these sisters a huge miracle of healing of a couple of the infirm sisters happened through the Infant Mary's intercession –and when this happened, lively color returned to the faded image. There is now a great church dedicated to the Infant Mary in that place. In November 1984, Pope John Paul II made a pilgrimage to this convent Church saying to the Sisters of Charity of Milan at their Motherhouse, *"This mystery [of the Holy Childhood of Mary] seems to be very little known. I think you have a great task........ to deepen the appreciation of the mystery of Mary's childhood."*

An Apparition in Mexico

Devotion to the Infant Mary sprang up as well in 1840 in Mexico City to a sister who knew nothing about these churches and statues in Milan. On January 6, 1840, the Feast of the Epiphany of Our Lord, Sister Magdalena de San José, a Franciscan Conceptionist sister, knelt before a nativity scene in her convent in Mexico City, contemplating the Christ Child in the manger. An inspiration came to her during her prayers that if there would be a similar devotion that will be accorded to the Child Mary. Suddenly, a lovely little girl appeared before her, dressed like a tiny princess and reclining in thin air. Sister Magdalena immediately knew that this beautiful child was the Virgin Mary, appearing to her in the form of a baby. The Infant Mary spoke to her giving her promise to those who will have a devotion to her Childhood: *"I will grant great graces to whoever honors me in my infancy"*.

The astonished nun went to the abbess and told her of her vision and her desire to promote devotion to little Mary. The abbess did not quite share Sister Magdalena's excitement, so the devotion was not promoted right away. But Sister Magdalena kept praying for God to bring it about. Eventually, Sister Magdalena did receive permission to ask a local sculptor to fashion a statue of the Infant Mary. Once she received the image she began to spread the devotion. Many people experienced miracles through the intercession of little Mary, but others questioned the suitability of such a devotion. Yet after years of careful study, Pope Gregory XVI approved the devotion and even granted indulgences to those who practiced it in 1846.

Devotion to the Child Mary in Malta

Another famed Shrine dedicated to the Child Mary was located in Senglea, Malta where the Child Mary became the focal point of the Maltese devotions. The origin of the statue dated back in 1618 where according to pious tradition, a statue of Our Lady was found floating together with other wreckage from a galleon (sailing ship), A captain of an Austrian galley, on reaching the vicinity of those islands, caught sight of the statue floating among the wreckage and fished it out of the sea, donating it to the nearest island which was Senglea in Malta. The devotion to the Child Mary in Senglea was strong in the area, most especially during the month of September. The devotion to the Infant Mary is also very popular in the Philippines, having been brought there by Spanish Missionaries.

The devotion of the Saints

Besides the revelations concerning Our Lady's infancy to several mystics and saints in the Church, there have been several other saints particularly devoted to Our Lady in Her Infancy. St. John Eudes wrote a beautiful Litany to the Infant Mary. St. Padre Pio and St. Joseph of Cupertino had a statue of the Maria Bambina in their private oratories. St. Hannibal Mary Di Francia of the Rogationist Order loved the child Mary with an ardent love and saw to it that in all his houses, She was venerated with special devotion. At the hour of his death, the Blessed Lady wanted to give him a sign of Her heavenly approval to the devotion. One morning, a few days before his death, his face suddenly lit up and he stared out a point in the room, exclaiming as though rapt: *"Brother, look!... Look how beautiful She is! Look at the beautiful Child Mary!..."* And he remained engrossed in the sweet vision.

Another foundress saint was known for her devotion to the Child Mary, notably Saint Jeanne de Lestonnac of the Order of the Company of Mary. Saint Jeanne was known for her active propagation to the devotion to the Child Mary by placing images of the Niña in the schools that were administered by her religious congregation. These schools held devotional activities like processions and other Marian devotions every November 21st, the Feast of the Presentation of Mary since 1610 when she initiated this tradition in the first school opened in Bordeaux, France. To express gratitude to God for all that had been accomplished in spite of difficulties and for the students to offer their lives to the Lord through the intercession of Mary, it was Saint Jeanne's wish that this feast be celebrated in all Company of Mary schools for all time and that it become a permanent tradition. This tradition was carried over to Vigo, Spain and in Japan where the Company of Mary also established their schools in those countries.

The Infant Mary as a Model for All

Devotion to the Maria Bambina (the Infant Mary) remains with us today as a model and inspiration for all –both children and adults alike. This sweet, little Immaculate One is a mighty intercessor against all evil. Her Heart is a Star to light our way to heaven. Her Heart is the voice of purity interceding for us before God. Her tiny Heart is a fortress against evil because of its purity. Her dedication to God is full through and through. Mary's 'Fiat' to the Angel in the Annunciation is not something new to Her –for She prayed 'Fiat' all of the days of Her life, even up unto (and through) the Cross with Her Son Jesus. In the midst of the greatest evil of the Passion and Death of Jesus, Her innocence and faith intercede for us before God. Her Love is stalwartly and resilient through all pain and death.

Our Lady was conceived in perfect purity and preserved that perfect purity by never choosing sin. In this She is a great example for all children as they progress through life to remain faithful in their commitment to God, no matter how they grow and mature into adults. She is an example for adults, inspiring us to return to littleness, humility and pure love in all we say and do –in how we pray –in how we interact with heaven and those we encounter on earth.

CHAPTER 2
Who is the Maria Bambina (Infant Mary)?

The Immaculate Virtue of the Infant Mary's Heart

We already spoke about the history of the devotion to the Maria Bambina –the Infant Mary. Yet why are we choosing in this book to specifically consecrate ourselves to Her under this title of Our Little Queen? The beauty, importance, power and grace in devotion to the Infant Mary comes from Her Immaculate Heart that was perfectly pure and always humble from the first moments of Her conception. What is emphasized here in Her littleness is the essence of the secret of Her place before God. Mary in Herself always was and always will be little, humble, weak and pure in the hands of Her Father. Nothing sullied Her Heart. It is because of Her littleness, purity, humility and weakness that the Father was able to possess Her being completely with the furnace of His Love in the Holy Spirit and that He was able to do such great things for Her and through Her. She was the first to proclaim this fact in the Magnificat when She prayed:

"My soul proclaims the greatness of the Lord and my spirit rejoices in God my Savior. For He has looked with great mercy on my lowliness. From henceforth, all generations will call me blessed. For the Almighty One has done great things for me and holy is His Name... He has lifted up the lowly... "

St. Louis de Montfort in 'True Devotion to Mary' writes:

"It was through the Blessed Virgin Mary that Jesus came into the world, and it is also through Her that He must reign in the world.

Because Mary remained hidden during Her life She is called by the Holy Ghost and the Church '"Alma Mater,' Mother hidden and unknown. So great was Her humility that She desired nothing more upon earth than to remain unknown to Herself and to others, and to be known only to God.

In answer to Her prayers to remain hidden, poor and lowly, God was pleased to conceal Her from nearly every other human creature in Her conception, Her birth, Her life, Her mysteries, Her resurrection and assumption. Her own parents did not really know Her and the angels would often ask one another, 'Who can She possibly be?' for God had hidden Her from them, or if He did reveal anything to them, it was nothing compared with what He withheld.

God the Father willed that She should perform no miracle during Her life; at least no public one, although He had given Her the power to do so. God the Son willed that She should speak very little although He had imparted his wisdom to Her;

Even though Mary was His faithful spouse, God the Holy Ghost willed that His apostles and evangelists should say very little about Her and then only as much as was necessary to make Jesus known.

Mary is the supreme masterpiece of Almighty God and He has reserved the knowledge and possession of Her for Himself. She is the glorious Mother of God the Son who chose to humble and conceal Her during Her lifetime in order to foster Her humility. He called Her 'Woman' as if She were a stranger, although in His heart He esteemed and loved Her above all men and angels. Mary is the sealed fountain and the faithful spouse of the Holy Ghost where only He may enter. She is the sanctuary and resting place of the Blessed Trinity where God dwells in greater and more divine splendor than anywhere else in the universe, not excluding His dwelling above the cherubim and seraphim. No creature, however pure, may enter there without being specially privileged..."

Our Lady was lifted so high in heaven because on earth She was the Queen of Humility. In the **Dialogue** God the Father says to St. Catherine of Siena: ***"Do you know daughter, who you are and who I am? If you know these two things you have beatitude in your grasp. You are she who is not, I AM HE WHO IS."*** Humility is simply the truth about ourselves and the truth about God. Our Lady always lived this truth. She was so united to Truth that in the Annunciation Truth Incarnate became flesh within Her –Jesus (Truth Incarnate) took His Flesh from Her Flesh. Jesus, Who said *"I am the Way, the Truth and the Life"* took life from Mary's Fiat. If Our Lady was given the honor of being the Mother of Truth Incarnate, then She was first the Queen of Humility. Only a Heart perfectly empty of Herself and full of God could be so consumed by God that He would take flesh within Her.

Mary's Humility is clear as we meditate on Her perfection even as an Infant. Her Humility placed Her as a creature, yet possessed and carried always by the Hand of God. Her weakness was a place for His Strength. Her surrender, trust, obedience and love –even as a small child –was the ember used by the Father to enkindle the Fire of the Holy Spirit's Love in Her Heart. Her eyes –crystal clear in their vision of things eternal –peered on this world through the perspective of Divine Wisdom and Love. She is called the 'Seat of Wisdom' and 'wisdom' means 'a listening heart'. She was always attentive to God –listening with Her entire being to His Heartbeat of Love and will so that She could fulfill it. And Our Lady as an Immaculate example of humility, purity, wisdom, trust, obedience and love wants to form us –Her children –to be imitators of Her foundation of virtue.

St. Louis de Montfort in 'True Devotion to Mary' writes:

"God the Holy Ghost wishes to fashion His chosen ones in and through Mary. He tells Her, 'My well-beloved, My spouse, let all your virtues take root in My chosen ones that they may grow from strength to strength and from grace to grace. When you were living on earth, practicing the most sublime virtues, I was so pleased with you that I still desire to find you on earth without your ceasing to be in heaven. Reproduce yourself then in My chosen ones, so that I may have the joy of seeing in them the roots of your invincible faith,

profound humility, total mortification, sublime prayer, ardent charity, your firm hope and all your virtues. You are always My spouse, as faithful, pure and fruitful as ever. May your faith give Me believers, your purity, virgins; your fruitfulness, elect and living temples.' When Mary has taken root in a soul She produces in it wonders of grace which only She can produce: for She alone is the fruitful virgin who never had and never will have Her equal in purity and fruitfulness...'

He continues:

"...Almighty God and His holy Mother are to raise up great saints who will surpass in holiness most other saints as much as the cedars of Lebanon flower above little shrubs... these great souls filled with grace and zeal will be chosen to oppose the enemies of God who are raging on all sides. They will be exceptionally devoted to the Blessed Virgin. Illumined by Her light, strengthened by Her food guided by Her spirit, supported by Her arm, sheltered under Her protection they will fight with one hand and build with the other. With one hand they will give battle, overthrowing and crushing heretics and other heresies, schismatics and their schisms, idolaters and their idolatries sinners and their wickedness. With the other hand they will build the temple of the true Solomon and the mystical city of God, namely, the Blessed Virgin, who

is called by the Fathers of the Church the Temple of Solomon and the City of God. By word and example they will draw all men to a true devotion to Her and though this will make many enemies, it will also bring about many victories and much glory to God alone... This is what was revealed to St. Vincent Ferrer... "

Mary has always been the Teacher of the saints. St. Faustina wrote, *"Mary is my Instructress, who is ever teaching me how to live for God. My spirit brightens up in Your gentleness and Your humility, O Mary."* (*Diary*, 620).

And in *Diary* entry 1711 St. Faustina reports:

*"When I was left alone with the Blessed Virgin she instructed me in the interior life. She said **"The soul's true greatness lies in loving God and in humbling oneself in His presence, completely forgetting oneself and believing oneself to be nothing; because the Lord is great, but He is well-pleased only with the humble; he always opposes the proud.""***

In *Diary* entry 1415, Mary gave to Faustina a message that focused on the importance of three virtues above all. Mary said to her:

"I desire, my dearly beloved daughter, that you practice the three virtues that are dearest to Me - and most pleasing to God. The first is humility, humility, and once again humility; the second virtue, purity; the third virtue, love of God. As my daughter, you must especially radiate with these virtues."

Small infants are naturally full of so many virtues –especially humility, docility, trust, purity and love. These virtues present in all small children were present in Mary in absolute perfection from the very beginning. As we grow in our own purification in virtue, we grow to imitate the perfect virtue resplendent as brilliant diamonds within Her Infant Heart.

St. Louis de Montfort in 'True Devotion to Mary' writes:

"What will they be like, these servants, these slaves, these children of Mary?

They will be ministers of the Lord who, like a flaming fire, will enkindle everywhere the fires of divine love. They will become in Mary's powerful hands, like sharp arrows, with which she will transfix her enemies. They will be as the children of Levi, thoroughly purified by the fire of great tribulations and closely joined to God. They will carry the gold of love in their heart, the frankincense of prayer in their mind and the myrrh of mortification in their body. The will bring to the poor and lowly everywhere the sweet fragrance of

Jesus, but they will bring the odor of death to the great, the rich and the proud of this world.

They will be like thunder-clouds flying through the air at the slightest breath of the Holy Ghost. Attached to nothing, surprised at nothing, troubled at nothing, they will shower down the rain of God's word and of eternal life. They will thunder against sin, they will storm against the world, they will strike down the devil and his followers and for life and for death, they will pierce through and through with the two-edged sword of God's word all those against whom they are sent by Almighty God.

They will be true apostles of the latter times to whom the Lord of Hosts will give eloquence and strength to work wonders and carry off glorious spoils from his enemies. They will sleep without gold or silver and, more important still, without concern in the midst of other priests, ecclesiastics and clerics. Yet they will have the silver wings of the dove enabling them to go wherever the Holy Ghost calls them, filled as they are with the resolve to seek the glory of God and the salvation of souls. Wherever they preach, they will leave behind them nothing but the gold of love, which is the fulfillment of the whole law.

Lastly, we know they will be true disciples of Jesus Christ, imitating his poverty, his humility, his contempt of the world and his love. They will point out the narrow way to God in pure truth according to the holy Gospel, and not according to the maxims of the world. Their hearts will not be troubled, nor will they show favor to anyone; they will not spare or heed or fear any man, however powerful he may be. They will have the two-edged sword of the word of God in their mouths and the blood-stained standard of the Cross on their shoulders. They will carry the crucifix in their right hand and the rosary I their left, and the holy names of Jesus and Mary on their heart. The simplicity and self-sacrifice of Jesus will be reflected in their whole behavior. Such are the great men who are to come. By the will of God Mary is to prepare them to extend his rule over the impious and unbelievers. But when and how will this come about? Only God knows..."

The Name of Mary

We see a small glimpse of the Father's Love for the Blessed Mother in the name She was given: Mary. The Blessed Mother's name is multifaceted. Some translations say it means, "*wished for child*" (a child not only 'wished for' by Anna and Joachim, but by all of humanity). Mary longed for the Messiah, but Israel longed for Her to give the Messiah.

The Latin translation of Mary from the Hebrew means, "*Sea, Star, "Drop of the Sea".* St. Jerome (writing c. 390), following Eusebius of Caesarea, translates the name as "drop of the sea" (*stella maris* in Latin), from Hebrew מר *mar* "drop" (cf. Isaias 40:15) and ים *yam* "sea" This translation was subsequently rendered *stella maris ("star of the sea")* due to scribal error, whence Our Lady's title Star of the Sea. Both reflect her identity –both as the sea of love that quenches Jesus' thirst and the sea that we travel to reach heaven (for She is the one who gave us Jesus who opened the gates of heaven to us for eternity). Mary is also our star, lighting the way in earth's darkness pointing the way to Christ.

In Egyptian, Mary means "*Beloved.*" And in Hebrew, Mary means "*Bitterness*", while others translate it "rebelliousness" It is beautiful to think of how Our Lady took all bitterness of the Cross and made it all sweet for Jesus. And it was Mary who CRUSHED ALL REBELLIOUSNESS WITH FIAT!

Regardless of which etymology of Mary you embrace, it is widely known that the very name of Mary –given to Her at birth – is powerful against demons and before the throne of God.

St. Louis de Montfort speaks about this in his book, "Secret of the Rosary" in the Chapter 'The Sixteenth Rose':

"One day when St. Mechtilde was praying and was trying to think of some way in which she could express her love of the Blessed Mother better than she had done before, she fell into ecstasy. Our Lady appeared to her with the Angelic Salutation in flaming letters of gold upon Her bosom and said to her: 'My daughter, I want you to know that no one can please Me more than by saying the salutation which the Most Adorable Trinity sent to Me and by which He raised Me to the dignity of Mother of God.

*"By the word **Ave** (which is the name Eve, Eva), I learned that in His infinite power God had preserved Me from all sin and its attendant misery which the first woman had been subject to.*

*"The name **Mary**, which means 'lady of light' shows that God has filled Me with wisdom and light, like a shining start, to light up heaven and earth.*

*"The words **full of grace** remind Me that the Holy Spirt has showered so many graces upon Me that I am able to give these graces in abundance to those who ask for them through Me as Mediatrix.*

*"When people say **The Lord is with thee** they renew the indescribable joy that was Mine when the Eternal Word became incarnate in My womb.*

*"When you say to Me **blessed art thou among women** I praise Almighty God's divine mercy which lifted Me to this exalted plane of happiness.*

*"And at the words **blessed is the fruit of thy womb, Jesus**, the whole of heaven rejoices with Me to see My Son Jesus Christ adored and glorified for having saved mankind."*

St. Maximillian Kolbe quoted in the 'Will to Love' on the power of Her Name as well:

"One 'Mary' spoken within the darkness, aridity and unhappiness of sin reechoes in Her heart, so much does She love

us! And the more unhappy a soul is, the more diligently She cares for it, for She is the Refuge of Sinners. And never worry that you do not sense this love. As long as you already want to love, that is a certain sign, in itself, that you do love, for love is a matter of the will. External feelings are also a fruit of grace, but these do not always follow immediately upon the action of the will. Sometimes you will find a sad nostalgia coming over you, a kind of pleading or complaint: 'Does not he Immaculata still love me?' My dearly beloved children, I say to each and every one of you individually in Her name – remember what I say –in Her name –She loves each and every one of you and She loves you at every moment without exception. This I repeat to you, my dear children, in Her name."

Reflections:

Holy Infant Mary, *pray for us.*
Infant Daughter of the Father, *pray for us.*
Infant, Mother of the Son, *pray for us.*
Infant, Spouse of the Holy Ghost, *pray for us.*
Infant, Sanctuary of the Holy Trinity, *pray for us.*

Mary says, **"I am the Queen Immaculate Conception –and this is a title that I bore from My birth, from My very conception in the womb of My mother. To call Me the 'holy' Infant Mary is to recognize that even from the first moments of My life hidden** away in My mother's womb, I was set aside as a gift for God and as the gift of God for the world. My Heart was created as the Perfect Garden of Paradise where the Word of God would take flesh and dwell –remaining united as one with My Heart through Love for all of eternity. To be called 'holy' means that I was a perfect Tabernacle of Grace, the 'Sanctuary of the Holy Trinity.' As the Daughter of the Heavenly Father I fulfilled His will for all women, for all of humanity, by always remaining surrendered and living a 'Fiat' in union with Him. As the Spouse of the Holy Spirit My entire being was inebriated with His Presence, consumed by the Spirit's Love as wood is combusted by fire, transformed completely as a creature divinely united to Her God. It is only because of this that I could become the 'Mother of the Son,' the 'Mother of the Eternal Word.'"

Infant, fruit of the prayers of thy parents, *pray for us.*
Infant, riches of thy father, *pray for us.*
Infant, delight of thy mother, *pray for us.*
Infant, honor of thy father, *pray for us.*
Infant, honor of thy mother, *pray for us.*
Most holy in thy Nativity, *pray for us.*
Most devout in thy Presentation, *pray for us.*

Mary says, "Before I was the 'Mother of the Son,' I was the human daughter of Sts. Anna and Joachim. I came forth into this world in the womb of prayer –as the fruit of their life of prayer and virtue together –as a surprise gift of the Father in their later years. The longing they offered to God for a child was the bed of suffering upon which My little life was laid –and it was this source of great purity and trust that was interwoven together with the heavenly virtue impressed within My little Heart. I was the pearl of great price –the only true riches of My Father's house. And I was the greatest delight of My Mother –who foresaw within My sudden appearance within her womb the hand of almighty God predestining Me to a great mission. I was therefore the honor of My parents –and they found their favor with God written upon the lines of My skin, in the innocence of My gaze, in the sweetness of My breath and the in the song of My Heart. I was holy in My conception and holy in My birth. And from the beginning My parents were aware that My life was a miracle of God created for God, and so they were joyful to offer Me back to Him in My Presentation. I was the first creature created by God to perfectly fulfill His will for My existence –to preserve completely My Heart created by God and for God in the pool of His Love."

Novena Prayer to the Maria Bambina (Infant Mary)

Holy Child Mary of the royal house of David, Queen of the angels,
Mother of grace and love, I greet you with all my heart.
Obtain for me the grace to love the Lord faithfully during
all the days of my life. Obtain for me, too, a great devotion
to you, who are the first creature of God's love.
Hail Mary, full of grace...............

O heavenly Child Mary, who like a pure dove was born
immaculate and beautiful, true prodigy of the wisdom of
God, my soul rejoices in you. Oh! Do help me to preserve
the angelic virtue of purity at the cost of any sacrifice.
Hail Mary, full of grace...............
Hail, lovely and holy Child, spiritual garden of delight, where,
on the day of the Incarnation, the tree of life was planted,
assist me to avoid the poisonous fruit of vanity and pleasures of
the world.
Help me to engraft into my soul the thoughts, feelings,
and virtues of your divine Son.
Hail Mary, full of grace...............
Hail, admirable Child Mary, Mystical Rose, closed garden,
open only to the heavenly Spouse. O Lily of paradise,
make me love the humble and hidden life;
let the heavenly Spouse find the gate of my heart always open
to the loving calls of His graces and inspiration.
Hail Mary, full of grace...............
Holy Child Mary, mystical dawn, gate of heaven,
you are my trust and hope.
O powerful advocate, from your cradle stretch out your hand,
support me on the path of life.
Make me serve God with ardor and
constancy until death and so reach an eternity with you.
Hail Mary, full of grace...............

Prayer:

Blessed Child Mary, destined to be the Mother of God and our loving Mother, by the heavenly graces you lavish upon us, mercifully listen to my supplications. In the needs which press upon me from every side and especially in my present tribulation, I place all my trust in you.

O holy Child, by the privileges granted to you alone and by the merits which you have acquired, show that the source of spiritual favors and the continuous benefits which you dispense are inexhaustible, because your power with the Heart of God is unlimited.

Deign through the immense profusion of graces with which the Most High has enriched you from the first moment of your Immaculate Conception, grant me, O Celestial Child, my petition, and I shall eternally praise the goodness of your Immaculate Heart.

IMPRIMATUR
In Curia Archiep. Mediolani
31 August 1931
Can. CAVEZZALI, Pro Vic. Gen

CHAPTER 3
Who is the Mystical Rose –Desert Rose?

St. Ildephonsus –**Crown of the Virgin Mary** in Chapter 13 'The Rose of Spring' writes:

"O Queen Divinely consecrated, you are nothing less than a seraphic throne from which shines forth with refulgent splendor the entire majesty, glory, virtue, and magnificence of the Holy Trinity! ...

...When you were born, O Virgin, you arose like a glowing dawn. For your birth marked the beginning of the day of grace and the end of the dark night of sin and infidelity. And you indeed possessed the beauty of the moon, filled with the grace of the conception of the incarnate Word. You brought forth the Sun of justice, Jesus Christ, and so you yourself were the morning of our salvation, putting to flight the darkness of our sin. And just as the ray departing from the sun does not diminish its coruscant brilliance –so, the Sun of justice and the Son of God being born from you did not violate or diminish our virginal purity. Through you, O Mother of mercy, the eternal rays of Divine splendor shone forth to the whole world!

And you are indeed like an army, arrayed for battle, for you appeared with all the angels exulting, all the saints rejoicing, all the flags of virtue flying. All the stars of the heavens stand ready and obedient at your behest.

O Lady miraculous –resplendent with the brilliance of the sun, exquisite with the loveliness of the moon! Accept the rose of spring which I offer you, that it may be positioned in the twelfth place in your noble coronet. For the rose is called the 'flower of flowers' for its surpassing excellence. It is pleasing to the sight, entrancing in its fragrance, and powerful in its medicinal properties. And all of these properties are to be found in you, O gracious Virgin.

But you are not merely like the earthly rose –which springs up and then soon withers. ***Rather, you are the rose of paradise, which is held lovingly in the hand of the King of heaven! For you are the perfect bloom of virginal beauty and the Queen of all virgins, the Empress of all holy maidens unmatched in radiance and peerless in immortal chastity.*** *And as you sit, triumphant, upon a sublime throne of imperial dignity. For you are of matchless beauty –in the sight of God, through your faith; and in the sight of angels, through your purity; and in the sight of sinful mortals, through your compassionate mercy.*

It was, indeed, the fragrance of your vernal sweetness that caused the Son of God himself to descend from his heavenly throne to this earthly realm. It was your perfection that compelled him to dwell as a guest in your virginal womb. And so a devout poet once fittingly wrote:

The sun outshines the moon, and the moon surpasses the stars;

Even so, Mother Mary exceeds all other created beings.

Hail, Mother of mercy! Hail, abode of the Trinity!

For Thou hast prepared within thyself the dwelling place of Christ himself, the home of the Word incarnate, the resting place of the Son of God.

Your healing power helps us in our infirmity and adversity, refreshes us in our labors, and consoles us in all sorrow. Indeed, it is said truly that your mercy, O Holy Virgin, is our surest aid in all peril and our best defense against all affliction.

Since you are graced with such a multitude of heavenly privileges, illumine –O most beautiful Light –my vision. Thus may I behold more clearly thy beauty! Heal my taste, that I may taste thy sweetness; renew my smelling that I may experience thy fragrance. Inflame my heart with thy most holy wisdom, that I may contemplate thee with wonder, love thee with fervor, venerate thee with true devotion, and cling to thee with fidelity!

Stand by me, O Lady, while I pray to you devoutly, and meditate upon you, and read about you, and speak of you and anxiously send up my sighs to you. For your perfume refreshes me. The thought of you brings me comfort, and your sweetness restores me. Your very presence consoles me. And your guidance faithfully leads me along the narrow path and straight road which leads to the divine light of heaven. Amen." -St. Ildephonsus

St. Louis de Montfort –"The Secret of the Rosary" –Chapter 'The Twenty-First Rose':

> *The works of Jesus and Mary can also be called wonderful flowers; but their perfume and beauty can only be appreciated by those who study them carefully –and who open them and drink in their scent by diligent and sincere meditation.*
>
> *"St Dominic has divided up the lives of Our Lord and Our Lady into fifteen mysteries which stand for their virtues and their most important actions. These are the fifteen tableaux or pictures whose every detail must rule and inspire our lives. They are fifteen flaming torches to guide our steps throughout this earthly life.*
>
> *They are fifteen shining mirrors which help us to know Jesus and Mary and to know ourselves as well. They will also help light the fire of their love in our hearts.*
>
> *They are fifteen fiery furnaces which can consume us completely in their heavenly flames... These re the fifteen fragrant flowers of the Mystical Rose Tree; devout souls fly to them like wise bees, so as to gather their nectar and make the honey of a solid devotion."*

And as the rose reigns by universal consent as the lovely queen of flowers, so Mary, the Woman clothed with the sun, which is charity, shines as the fairest flower in God's garden and is acclaimed as the "Mystical Rose."

We find the most beautiful meditation on Our Lady as Rosa Mystica in the writings of Saint Brigid:

"The rose," Mary told Saint Brigid, *"gives a fragrant odor; it is beautiful to the sight, and tender to the touch, and yet it grows among thorns, inimical to the beauty and tenderness. So may also those who are mild, patient, beautiful in virtue, be put to a test among adversaries. And as the thorn, on the other hand, guards, so do wicked surroundings protect the just against sin by demonstrating to them the destructiveness of sin."* Saint Brigid then added: *"The Virgin may suitably be called a blooming rose. Just as the gentle rose is placed among thorns, so this gentle Virgin was surrounded by sorrow."*

St. Ambrose relates how the rose came to have thorns. Before it became one of the flowers of the earth, the rose grew in Paradise without thorns. Only after the fall of man did the rose take on its thorns to remind man of the sins he had committed and his fall from grace; whereas its fragrance and beauty continued to remind him of the splendor of Paradise. It is probably in reference to this that the Virgin Mary is called a 'rose without thorns,' because she was exempt from Original Sin.

Holy Rosary

As you already imagine, the Holy Rosary, of course, takes its name from the Rose. The word Rosary means "Crown of Roses." Roses are a symbol of the Rosary and its mysteries. Rosebuds are a figure of Jesus as Infant; half-blown blossoms represent the Passion of Christ. The full flower shows forth Christ's victory over death and triumph. Similarly, the different colors and parts of the rose bush should remind us of the Joyful, Sorrowful, and Glorious mysteries. And, since Mary is herself called Mystical Rose, she obtains for us the blessing attached to the blessed roses.

In addition, Saint Louis de Montfort, in his book, The *Secret of the Rosary*, speaks symbolically of the White Rose of purity, simplicity, devotion; the Red Rose of the Precious Blood of Our Lord. He also speaks of the Rose Tree, symbolizing the Mystical Roses of Jesus and Mary. He compares the rosebud to a rosary bead, and urges children to regard the prayers of the rosary as "your little wreath of roses for Jesus and Mary." In short, "a rose delights us because of its beauty----so we have Jesus and Mary in the Joyous Mysteries. Its thorns are sharp, and pricks, which makes us think of them in the Sorrowful Mysteries, and last of all its perfume is so sweet that everyone loves it, and this fragrance symbolizes their Glorious Mysteries."

As early as the 4th century, St. Gregory of Naziansus spoke of "weaving a chaplet for the Virgin Mary." Chaplet here means the same thing as crown or wreath. Further, according to 13th-century

German and Spanish legends, a monk saw the "aves" (Hail Marys) he offered to Mary turn into a chain of roses. These Hail -Marys-seen-as-roses would be rendered into English as the Rosary. Pope Leo XIII will go on to say, *"For as often as we greet Mary with the angelic salutation, 'full of grace,' we present to the Blessed Virgin, in the repetition of our words of praise, roses which emit the most delightful perfume."* Each prayer offered through Mary takes on the sense of a rose being lovingly arranged. As Pope Pius XII would say, among the many things the rose represents, we should interpret them as manifestations of *"the fullness of her perfections and the delicacy of her goodness."*

St. Bernard wrote, ***"Eve was a thorn, wounding, bringing death to all. In Mary we see a rose, soothing everybody's hurts, giving the destiny of salvation back to all."*** A rose's thorns could also stand for Her sacrifice in accepting the role of Mother of God.

According to Cardinal John Henry Newman, the Blessed Virgin Mary is called *Rosa Mystica, the Mystical Rose,* because she ***"is the Queen of spiritual flowers; and therefore She is called the Rose, for the rose is fitly called of all flowers the most beautiful."*** That would explain the name "rose" but Newman asks the reason for the adjective "hidden." His reply is that Her tomb was not to be found on earth as that of the saints and martyrs. *"Is it conceivable that they who had been so reverent and careful of the bodies of the Saints and Martyrs should neglect Her—Her who was the Queen of Martyrs and the Queen of Saints, who was the very Mother of our Lord? It is impossible. Why then is She thus* *the* hidden *Rose? Plainly because that sacred body is in heaven, not on earth."*

Desert Rose...

Our Lady could also be called a Desert Rose. Our Lady was not spoiled in a lush garden with an 'easy life' (even spiritually). No - Her life was for the desert. Her life was the narrow way spoken of by Her Son. Her life was step by step after Him -following His bloody footprints. Her life was His way of the Cross. But, *'In the place where Jesus was crucified there was a garden.'* (John 19:41) God wanted desert fruit from Mary. A desert rose is not a small flower –it is actually a huge tree that grows in the desert. He wanted a neglected plant without water and sun to grow huge and indestructible because of His Grace (for 'His Grace alone is sufficient for me' (2 Corinthians 12:9)) and then to give forth tons of little flowers in the end. In Isaiah 35:1 It says that it is the desert (and not the lush garden) that springs forth flowers... *__"The wilderness and the dry land shall be gladdened; and the desert shall rejoice, and blossom as the rose."__*

In the years Mary spent as a child in the temple, She learned about the Israelites longing for a Savior and She made Her people's thirst Her Own. From the moment of the Incarnation, Our Lady made the Cross that was to be Her Son's lot in life Her own. She suffered misunderstanding by all around Her –even Joseph planned to divorce Her quietly until the angel of the Lord appeared to Him. She joyfully took on the burden of traveling far on foot (even in Her expecting condition) to take care of Elizabeth, little John the Baptist and Zachariah. She gave birth in a cave –rejected from inns –and had to flee into Egypt. She heard Simeon in the temple prophesize the future suffering of Her little Son and She watched Him bleed in the circumcision. She lost Him for three days in the temple and then in His public ministry watched Him misunderstood, rejected, mocked, abandoned and hated by so many for His Goodness. Ultimately She watched Him suffer a hideous Passion –torture from man and satan alike –and then murdered on the Tree of the Cross. Our Lady's life was anything but easy –yet Her virtue, holiness, purity and love shone forth as a great river of beauty in the midst of it all. In this She truly was a marvelous Rose Tree blooming in a desert of this world's sin.

A real Desert Rose Tree is not small –it grows to be 10 feet tall. They are giants in the desert. The root system is complicated, thick and deep- just like the deep, strong root system of Our Lady's interior life. Desert Rose Trees have a very special value to bees. Honey (sweetness) comes from a tough desert flower-tree. This is like Our Lady –as She kept Her Heart resting in God's hand and united to His Heart on the Cross, therefore She could give others His sweet drink of Love and Mercy no matter what She Herself was suffering.

A desert rose tree is a plant that grows best when neglected... so often Our Lady's only source of consolation and spiritual help came from God's Presence Himself within Her. Her Virtue towered most strongly as She stood alone at the foot of the Cross –in the midst of Calvary's night She was entrusted with the responsibility of being the Mother of the entire Church when John was handed to Her.

One more funny thing is that the sap of a desert rose tree contains toxic cardiac glycosides and is used as arrow poison throughout Africa for hunting large game. In a similar way, it is the 'sap' of Mary's Love union with God that poisons satan –it is through Her Fiat surrender to Him in everything that the head of the evil one is crushed forever.

Reflections:

Mystical rose, *pray for us.*
Tower of David, *pray for us.*
Tower if ivory, *pray for us.*
House of gold, *pray for us.*
Gate of heaven, *pray for us.*
Ark of the covenant, *pray for us.*
Pattern of our charity, *pray for us.*
Model of our humility, *pray for us.*

Mary says, '**I am the Mystical Rose. The word 'mystical' means 'hidden,' and My being has been hidden in perfection in the mind of God from the beginning of eternity. I was the eternal blueprint for women –and for all of humanity in a way –for I was the only human to ever perfectly fulfill the will of God in all things at all times in all ways. Because of My Immaculate Conception I was forever without the obstacle of sin –even of original sin –which would stain the intention of all people who came before or after Me (with the exception of Jesus). I was that per-**

fect Flower that bloomed from the desert Heart of the will of God Who desired to come to earth to be crucified to save all. And because of this –because I was the 'Mother of the Savior' – being a Rose My life was not left without the pain of thorns. Suffering purified My Love and protected Me from the wiles of the enemy who was determined to deter Me from My resolute path of trust in the goodness and providence of My Heavenly Father. Yet the abyss of My virtue was hidden from the world in a simple, obscure life, and so because of this the depths of the fragrance of My Love was only detected in full by the Son of God until the time determined by the Father for Him to reveal it to the world. This was completed in full at the foot of the Cross when Jesus gave Me as Mother of the Church to St. John, and then entrusted this Apostle to My Motherly care. For this reason I can be called the 'Tower of David' –for I came as the lowliest of the family of David and yet was raised up as a Tower of Faith as I completed My Fiat at the Annunciation by a perfected Fiat on Calvary. *"For He has looked with favor on His Lowly servant... He has cast down the mighty from their thrones and has lifted up the lowly."* Because '*My soul proclaimed the greatness of the Lord and My spirit rejoiced in God My Savior...*" I could be called 'Tower of Ivory.' This foundation of humility and purity within My being allowed God to lift Me high as a Tower of Ivory –with the strength and whiteness that only comes from humility and purity. And in this embrace of His gift of perfect holiness to Me, He placed His Own Presence in the Incarnation –and therefore I can be called a 'Gate to Heaven' (for Heaven lived within Me) and a 'House of Gold' as well. The Arc of the Covenant was where the Law of God was kept –and since the greatest Law of God was that of Love –when Love became Incarnate within Me in Jesus, I became greater than the Arc of the Covenant of old. I was the breathing, fiating, loving Rose embracing and hiding God eternal within My Heart and Body. My entire being became a pattern of His charity. Usually a child resembles his parent, and yet in the case of little Jesus and Me, the Fire of His Love transformed Me to resemble Him. In this I was a model of humility –empty of Myself in order to be totally consumed and filled by God."

Infant, most powerful, *pray for us.*

Infant, most mild, *pray for us.*

Infant, most pure, *pray for us.*

Infant, most obedient, *pray for us.*

Infant, most poor, *pray for us.*

Infant, most meek, *pray for us.*

Infant, most amiable, *pray for us.*

Infant, most admirable, *pray for us.*

Infant, incomparable, *pray for us.*

Infant, our Mother, *pray for us.*

Purity of Virgins, *pray for us.*

Queen of all Saints, *pray for us.*

Infant, Queen of our hearts, *pray for us.*

Mary said, 'What is important for Me to draw your attention to is the fullness of this beauty and perfection of My Heart already in My infancy. **Because of the Immaculate Conception, the greatness of God was able to dwell completely in Me even as a baby. Only in such humility and purity filled by God's Love completely, could I be praised as an infant 'most powerful' –it was because in My utter weakness, God had room to grow His graces of strength and courage. His power could be alive in full in Me without any blockage from sin. It was because I was His 'Infant, most mild, pure, obedient, poor, meek and amiable' that He could fill Me with His Divinity making Me 'most admirable, incomparable and Queen.' In My lowliness I became the perfect Mother of Humanity and the Purity of all Virgins. By allowing Christ to reign in full within Me at all times, I became not only the Queen of all saints in heaven, but also the Queen of all hearts still on earth –even those struggling against sin and temptations. Being little and nothing Myself, God could raise Me to be the Queen Mother of all of mankind –simply by reigning through Love."**

<u>**Prayer to the Mystical Rose**</u> by Thomas Canon Pope

O Mary! Mystical Rose! I am in admiration of the agreeable and admirable odour of thy virtues, and, at the same time, I am overwhelmed with confusion and sorrow when I reflect on the garden of my own soul, in which I can discover no flower or fragrance of virtue, and in which I find nothing but the thorns and cockles of vices. Ah, obtain for me the grace that as, in former days, Francis turned into roses the thorns in which Benedict rolled himself, so, in like manner, the thorns of my sins may be converted into the roses of virtues; and, in token of my gratitude, I shall frequently crown thee with roses, which I shall effect by the devout recitation of the Rosary. O MARY!

Mystical Rose, Pray for us!

From The Illustrated Litany of Loretto (Published by James Duffy and Sons in 1878)

Star of the Stormy Sea

CHAPTER 4

Who is the Morning Star- Star of the Sea?

Lord God, redeemer and inspiration of souls,
in the Blessed Virgin Mary, Star of the Sea,
you have provided a light in the storm.
By Her favor and prayer,
grant that we may set a course through these times
to reach our safe haven in heaven with you.

(*Opening Prayer of the Mass of the Blessed Virgin Mary,*
Stella Maris)

St. John in the Apocalypse tells of the Woman Clothed with the Sun: *"On Her head was a crown of twelve stars."* So in art Our Lady is often picture as the Madonna of the Star. Stars are embroidered on Her veil or on the right shoulder of Her blue mantle. Art glorifies Her as the Morning Star, the Star of the Sea, the Star of Jacob, the Fixed Star.

As I already stated, Cardinal Newman writes, it is *"Mary's prerogative to be the Morning Star, which heralds in the sun. She does not shine for Herself, or from Herself, but She is the reflection of Her and our Redeemer, and She glorifies Him. When She appears in the darkness, we know that He is close at hand..."* Newman also compares the "Morning Star" to Mary's Assumption into heaven: *"Mary, like the stars, abides forever, as lustrous now as She was on the day of her Assumption; as pure and perfect, when Her Son comes to judgment, as She is now."*

St. Ildephonsus –*Crown of the Virgin Mary* in Chapter 15, "The Sun" writes:

"O Mary –unbroken seal of chastity, pure lily of virginity, most beautiful of women, more delightful than all the angels, more holy than all the saints, richer than all created being in abundance of grace! Seraphim hail you! God the Father sanctifies you, God the Holy Spirit shades you protectingly, God the Son chooses you as his betrothed! The sanctity of your soul conceived God through faith. The purity of your womb bore him. The Virginity of your body brought him forth into the world.

O glorious Lady! And more than glorious! O praise-worthy Virgin and more than praiseworthy! Who is able to express your wonders or worthily to tell of your merits? For you gave joy to heaven, you bore God himself to the earth, you opened the river of celestial peace to a troubled world. Through you, O Queen of heaven:

> *Light is given to the blind,*
> *Sure faith bestowed to doubtful hearts,*
> *Vices are brought under control,*
> *Demons are confounded,*
> *Ravenous hell is deprived of its prey.*
> *Heaven is enriched,*
> *The poor are nourished,*

The weak are sustained,
The humble are raised up
The gates of paradise are uncloaked.

Therefore the patriarchs long for you. The apostles embrace you. The Evangelists reverence you. The martyrs venerate you. The preachers proclaim your glory. The choirs of virgins rejoice around you. The angels glorify you, and all of creation exalts you! Even I –a lowly sinner –seek to contribute in some way to your glory and honor. And so I venture to offer to you the sun itself, the most radiant and potent of the celestial bodies, to be positioned in the fourteenth place in your noble crown. Thence it may freely shed its luster upon you, bathing you in incomparable light!

For the sun possess the highest position in the celestial sphere, and the greatest sureness in its daily motion across the sky. It brings forth the greatest fertility in its effect upon the earth, while bestowing the gift of light more brilliantly than any other star. **Similarly you, O mistress, are raised up most high of all, by virtue of your sanctity and singular purity. Your Immaculate Heart is raised up to the uppermost rank in the seraphic courts, closest to the inaccessible light of the unseen Father. With the gentle eyes of a dove you lovingly contemplate his luminous divinity. With the fearless and penetrating eyes of an eagle you boldly perceive the depths of his majesty. And your every action pro-**

ceeds with the greatest sureness –with unfailing certainty and assurance, born of true piety. Like the sun, you traverse the earthly globe, attentively beholding the needs of the poor, the anxious sighs of youth, the pains of the elderly, the lamentations of widows, the sufferings of the sick, and the prayers poured forth to you and your Holy Son from faithful hearts everywhere. As the gracious Protectress of the entire race, you help the afflicted, the sorrowful, and those who have lost hope. You do this by the divine grace of your mercy and by your powerful intercession with your noble Son, Jesus –the King of kings and the Lord of lords!

And –like the warming sun which causes the earth to flourish with springtide verdancy –so you make souls once barren to become fruitful. For who is able to moisten the dry heart like you? Or who is able to warm the mind, frozen with despair or cynicism? All the good things, which God's supreme Majesty has decreed to bestow on us, he has decreed to bestow through your intercession and agency. He has committed to your maternal hands the entire treasuries of his golden wisdom, the precious gemstones of his virtues, and the glowing ornaments of his graces. Through you –radiant as the sun, as gentle as the dawn –the fruits of blessings spring forth from their divine source.

How many are the former thieves you have led to repentance? How many are the reformed prostitutes you have converted to chastity? How many of the avaricious have you *made generous, and to how many drunkards have you taught sobriety? How many of the wrathful have you tempered by the example of your patience and mercy, and how many of the lustful have you restrained by the example of your immaculate purity?*

Utterly radiant and splendid you stand, clothed in light as with a vestment, and crowned with twelve glowing starts! As the refulgent sun dawns with golden radiance, so you adorn and illuminate the celestial Jerusalem, the city of paradise, the abode of saints, angels and God himself! And therefore the ranks of the angels are struck with wonder, and the legions of seraphim stand awestruck before you, O Mary! For you are indeed the very perfection of sanctity, the complete plenitude of grace, and the **luminous fire of God's ardent love.**

O Lady of Grace, since such marvels are told of Thee, pour forth, I beseech thee, thy love into my heart. Show unto me the angelic beauty of thy countenance, splendid as the noontide sun. Grant that, at the hour of my death, I may surrender my spirit –joyful in thy radiance, and secure in the hope of unfading glory. Amen.

St. Ildephonsus *'The Crown of Mary'* –chapter 7 'The Star Arcturus':

*"Most serene Queen and inviolate Mother of God –
Virgin pure, holy and immaculate –we praise your purity,
while we marvel at your humility. But even more lovingly –
for it is ever sweeter and more needful to the sinner –we invoke your mercy and clemency. Your perfume is the gift of
the Holy Spirit. This Spirit rests in you, illuminating you,
and inflaming you with his love. Your Fruit is truly eternal –
the fragrance of which fills the world, the taste of which delights the faithful heart, the splendor of which surpasses even
the sun and its noontide magnificence!*

*Because, therefore, as a rich and delicate vine you have
borne a Fruit so precious –Jesus Christ, our Lord to
acknowledge something of your glory and magnificence, in
the sixth position in your crown I place the star Arcturus.
This star is bright and luminous and decorated with seven
lesser stars. These seven lesser stars form around it a constellation in the image of a chariot or wagon. To this form, O
Mistress, you may –in a certain way –be compared. For you
are star-like in your purity and most dazzling in your faith
and sanctity. With seven stars –just as with seven virtues –
you are gloriously adorned.*

*For you were indeed strong through the virtue of faith,
brightly ablaze through the virtue of love, raised to the
heights through the virtue of hope. Through the virtue of
temperance, you were sober and modest. Through the virtue
of fortitude, you were most constant; through the virtue of*

justice, most equitable; and through the virtue of prudence, most wise.

And you indeed served as the chariot of God, carrying in your holy soul God Almighty, and holding in your sacred womb our Lord Jesus Christ. You are indeed the chariot of the true Israel; that is, the Church –kindly imploring peace and mercy for our sins and exhibiting the pathway which leads to paradise. My Mistress! Consolation of my heart, sweetness of my soul, refreshment of my spirit! Mercifully correct and amend my stony and beast-like ways. Through your merits, grant to me peace and forgiveness. Through your very self, let the way to paradise be revealed to me and let the doors of heaven be unbolted!

O Lady most illustrious, teach me what I may offer that would be pleasing to you. Demonstrate to me what I may present that would be acceptable, what gift I may give that would be worthy of your beauty and love. Parch the thirst of this contemptible sinner with the fruitful rain of your stainlessness; nourish this horrid worm with the richness of your sweetness. Rescue me from the dark forces which surround me, and confound those who would destroy my soul! May my spiritual enemies be dispersed like smoke and shadows. May they perish, crushed by your power, O great Lady. May the Inferno swallow them alive!

Open –O Key of David! –the depths of your honey-flowing heart. Open the gate of your immortal light, that I may enter and see, and taste the sweetness of your kiss, and that my thirsting soul may be inebriated by your most sweet gaze. Out of this miraculous refreshment, may I learn to love you with my whole heart and mind –fervently and prudently, sincerely and joyously, humbly and devoutly. Grant to me such a voice of exultant praise that I may fittingly proclaim your wonders!

Blessed is your flower-adorned chastity, and blessed is your virginal motherhood! Blessed is your gracious humility, and blessed is your heart-felt piety. Blessed is your unique sanctity by which you re rendered more excellent than all other created beings, and blessed is that special dignity by which you are rendered more precious than the entire created universe!

For the Holy Spirit –as a mellifluous dewfall from on high –made you conceive within your womb. Through a divine overshadowing, the Dove of heaven lovingly shaded your most holy body. The same Spirit indelibly signed your most blessed soul as the noble and unique resting place of the entire Trinity. Thus your spirit was adorned with the gold of faith, the silver of wisdom, the priceless gems of sanctity, the roses of modesty, the lilies of chastity, and the violets of virginity! Thus was your Immaculate Heart illuminated by the Sun of justice and made radiant by the moon of chastity and the stars of innocence. You were decorated with the orna-

ments of all graces and made unspeakably noble with the sacred anointing of perfect holiness.

O Virgin Lady, elevated and filled by so many and by such graces! May you be merciful to us in our needs, sweet in our tribulations, merciful in our anxieties, and quick to help in our perils. You indeed are the refuge of the troubled, the solace of the sorrowful. You gently wipe away the tears of those who mourn. We –your children –are pressed down by the weight of our sins, flooded by the turbulent waves of vain desire, and battered by the acrid waves of empty pleasures.

But, O, have mercy upon us! Lest we be enwrapped in perpetual darkness and consigned to eternal woe –help us in the hour of sadness and in the hour when fearful death draws nigh. Lead us to the bliss of the holy Resurrection and to the joy of immortal light! Amen."

Mary is the "*Stella Matutina,*" the Morning Star—after the Dark Night, but always heralding the Sun. She is at once the *Rosa Mystica* and the *Stella Matutina.* She is God's perfect, hidden Rose eternally exhaling the perfume of praise to God in heaven. And She is the Morning Star –a sign of the coming Day of Jesus –the Son of God –to earth. And a Guide through Her Light –like a Star on a Stormy Sea –pointing our way to our heavenly homeland. She does not shine for Herself, or from Herself, but She is the reflection of Her and our Redeemer, and She glorifies Him. When She appears in the darkness, we know that He is close at hand. Our Lady, as the Morning Star, goes ahead of Christ to announce the coming of His

Light. Her loving purpose is to prepare the way for Our Lord and reflect His glory: *"I am the root and the descendant of David, the bright morning star"* (Rev 22:16). She shines not of Herself, but reflects the brightness and glory of Our Lord.

Our Lady then, as the Morning Star, precedes the Son whose radiance She reflects and by Her presence She announces His coming. It is thus fitting to reflect upon just *how* Mary reflects this glory so that we can try to emulate Her as a pattern of holiness. We should always be mindful of Her presence in showing us the way to the Lord and let ourselves be so guided by Her to Him.

History of Our Lady's Title, 'The Morning Star- Star of the Sea'

Our Lady has been honored as the "Morning Star" and "Star of the Sea" as far back as the ninth century when the loveliest of hymns was written about Her—the ***Ave Maris Stella***, and then later on in the eleventh century when the ***Alma Redemptoris Mater*** appeared. The "Morning Star" has always had a special application to Mary. The Church interprets the verse in the Song of Songs as descriptive of Her. *"Who is She that cometh forth as the morning rising, fair as the moon, bright as the sun?"* Every church today, as in ages past, has its altar of the Blessed Virgin. In the old Cathedrals, the Lady Chapel was situated behind the choir and the high altar, and to the extreme east, as the symbol of Her as the Morning Star. We read in an old book of the 16th century: *"Like as the morn-*

ing cometh before the sun rising, and divideth the night from the day, so the Virgin Mary rose as the morning before the Sun of Justice, and divided the state of grace from the state of sin, the children of God from the children of darkness. Whereupon the Church singeth to Her praise that Her glorious life gave light to the world and illumined all the Church and congregations of faithful people." So a Solemn Mass was sung every day at early dawn in Her honor, and the bell for rising was called "Saint Mary's bell." St. Bridget of Sweden calls Her "the star preceding the sun."

The very thought of Light brings up the vision of Mary, so much had She to do with the Light of the world. Her arms were the candlestick for that Light. Candlemas, the Feast of Lights, is Her Feast, as She holds up to a darkened world the true Light. So, St. Epiphanius († 403) called Her *"Mother of Eternal Light."* In the Hymn for the Feast of the Guardian Angels She is also called "Mother of Light," and in the Hymn for the Feast of the Most Holy Rosary: *"Twelve stars now crown the brow of the glorious Mother; near the throne of Her Son She reigns over all created things."*

The Hymn *Quem terra* sings—She is the "refulgent hall of Light." She is also called "Light of the Despairing," "Daughter of the Light Unapproachable," "Our Light," "Bright Moon of Purity," "Brilliant Star of Purity," "Rising Moon of Purity," "Sun without a Stain," "Living Light of Holiness."

"Our Lady of Light" was an old title of Hers in the Middle Ages. It is said that She Herself suggested that title to St. Thomas of Canterbury. There was a Confraternity of Our Lady of Light, and St. Francis Xavier and his companions were enrolled in it before they set out for the Indies. The Confraternity of Our Lady of Light, Spouse of the Holy Ghost was founded in England, in 1824. Pope Leo XIII indulgenced this prayer: *"Our Lady of Light, Spouse of the Holy Ghost, I give Thee my whole self, soul and body, all I have or may have, to keep for Jesus that I may be His forever more. Our Lady of Light, Spouse of the Holy Ghost, pray for me."*

But the most common "Star" figure, which all the spiritual writers have used, is "Star of the Sea," the guide to man who is sailing on the sea of life. St. Bernard, as many others, interpreted *Miriam (Hebrew for "Mary")* as meaning *Star of the Sea*, and thus explains it: *"Because without loss of its own integrity, a star sends forth its rays—and so Mary brought forth Jesus. She is, therefore, that noble star risen out of Jacob, whose ray illuminates the whole earth, whose splendor both shines above and pierces the nether darkness, enlightening the earth and giving heat rather to souls than to bodies, nourishing virtues, expelling vices. Mary is the excellent, bright and wonderful Star lifted up necessarily above this great and wide ocean, shining with merits, illuminating with example. Behold the Star!"*

It is a strange thing, but almost all the figures of speech in Scripture about the sea refer to its power and its dangers. All dreaded the unknown sea. Having no compass in those days, many ships were lost in the great traffic on the Mediterranean. The sea has always had its dangers. The sailors knew that better than anyone else. A strange name the Eastern sailors gave Her—*Mother of Tears*, evidently because the sea made so many mothers weep for their lost sailor boys. But the Catholic sailor was devoted to the Star of the Sea. He needed Her protection in his dangerous calling, so he called his boat after one of Her titles, paid his homage to Her shrines along the coast, made vows of pilgrimage and of offering to Her. One of the most famous shrines of France is that of Our Lady of Mariners, at Marseilles. At the end of the 12th century a fisherman of Marseilles was overtaken in his boat by a violent storm. He raised his eyes to the rock of the Garde. He beheld a figure there. He sang the *Ave Maris Stella*. Somehow he got to land. Many sailors saw that same apparition on the rock. A chapel was erected and a statue was placed there, called "Our Lady of Help" or "Help of Mariners." Since then She is honored as the Protectress of Marseilles. Many stories are told of sailors in distress seeing Our Lady at the wheel guiding their boat through the storm. She was, indeed, "the Star above the storms."

Fr. Faber wrote a beautiful hymn with the idea of the Star of the Sea protecting us in our voyage of life —"Sweet Star of the Sea."

Deep night hath come down on us, Mother, deep night,
And we need more than ever the guide of Thy light;
For the darker the night is, the brighter should be
Thy beautiful shining, sweet Star of the Sea.

St. Bonaventure compares life to a tempestuous sea into which sinners have fallen from the ship of Divine Grace. *"O poor lost sinners,"* he makes Our Lady say, *"despair not; raise up your eyes and cast them on this beautiful star; breathe again with confidence, for it will save you from this tempest and will guide you into the port of salvation."*

And St. Ephraim calls Her *"the safe harbor of all sailing on the sea of the world,"* the same expression being used by Pope Leo XIII—*"Safe Harbor of travelers."* St. Thomas draws his lesson from it—*"She is blessed among women because She alone has removed the curse of Adam, brought blessings to mankind, and opened the gates of Paradise. Hence She is called Mary, which name signifies Star of the Sea, for as sailors steer their ship to port by watching the stars, so Christians are brought to glory by the intercession of Mary."*

Mary is compared to the merchant's ship, *"She brings Her bread from afar" (Prov. 31: 14).* So do we look up to Her—we who *"have walked in the waves of the sea" (Eccli. 24: 8).* Thus St. Gertrude the Great prayed, *"O Jesus, my only hope, my Savior and my God, send to me, at my last hour Thy tender Mother Mary, that soft-shining Star of the Sea, that She may stand by me as my sure defense. Her face, fair as the bright dawn of morning will make me feel and know that Thou, too, O Divine Sun of Justice, art drawing near to my soul in all Thy splendor."*

St. Bernard of Clairvaux had so much trust in Mary's powerful intercession that he said: *"God has wanted that we obtain nothing if not through the hands of Mary."* For St. Bernard *"Mary is our mediatrix"*; and we receive the Holy Spirit that *"overflows from her."* He says that *"Every soul, even though weighed down with sins, ensnared in vice, caught in the allurements of the passions, held captive in exile, and imprisoned in the body ... even, I say, though it be thus damned and in despair, can find within itself not only reasons for yearning for the hope of pardon and the hope of mercy, but also for making bold to aspire to the nuptials of the Word, not hesitating to establish a covenant of union with God, and not being ashamed to carry the sweet yoke of love along with the King of the Angels,"* like Mary.

In his *Praises of the Virgin* it is through Mary that Bernard describes the mystery of God and of man, and the mystery of the *Fiat* which gave beginning to the relationship between man and God, and is able to invade the Christian soul and impregnate it with God. In particular, there are two figures which help us say our own "Fiat" to God; the Virgin as Star and as divine Lover.

Mary is the guide for every man, and the guide for our history because in Her is found the perfect humanity. Because of this She is called the Star of the Sea. Because of Her presence of Love with us, children of God are no longer alone in their quest for God; they are not abandoned to the uncertainty of the sea waters in the dark night, for a firm point has appeared in heaven: it is the Mother. St. Bernard says:

"Whoever you are that perceive yourself during this mortal existence to be rather drifting in treacherous waters, at the mercy of the winds and the waves, than walking on firm ground, turn not away your eyes from the splendor of this guiding star, unless thou wish to be submerged by

the storm. ... Look at the star, call upon Mary. ... With her for guide, you shall not go astray, while invoking her, you shall never lose heart ... if she walks before you, you shall not grow weary; if she shows you favor, you shall reach the goal."

In a homily he further expressed his love and confidence in Our Lady as the Star of the Sea by writing this incredible prayer to Her:

"O Thou who feelest thyself tossed by the tempests in the midst of the shoals of this world, turn not away thine eyes from the Star of the Sea, if thou wouldst avoid shipwreck.

If the winds of temptation blow, if tribulations rise up like rocks before thee—look at the Star, send a sigh towards Mary!

If the waves of pride, ambition, calumny, or jealousy seek to swallow up thy soul—<u>look at the Star, send a prayer to Mary!</u>

If anger, avarice, or love of pleasure toss thy fragile bark— seek the eyes of Mary.

If horror of thy sins, trouble of conscience, or dread of the judgments of God begin to plunge thee into the gulf of sadness, the abyss of despair—attach thy heart to Mary.

In dangers, in sufferings, in doubt—think of Mary and invoke Her aid.

Let Mary be always in your heart and often upon your lips.

To obtain Her help in death, follow Her example in life.

In following Her, you will not go astray; by praying to Her, you will not despair; if you cling to Her, you will not go wrong. With Her support, you fall not; under Her protection you have no fear; under Her guidance you do not grow weary; if She is gracious to you, you will reach the port.

Thus you will experience how rightly it is said: 'And the Virgin's name was Mary'."

St. John Bosco, known for his prophetic and mystical dreams, also dreamt once of Our Lady as a great star guiding the ship of the Church (along with the Eucharist) to safety. In perhaps this -his most famous dream - he saw a large ship, representing the Church, in a violent storm and under attack. The Pope guided the ship to two large columns, at which, the ship docked and was saved. On the one column was a statue of the Virgin Mary with the title "the Help of Christians;" and, at the top of the other larger column was a Eucharist Host entitled "the Salvation of the Faithful." St. John Bosco explained: *"Only two means are left to save her amidst the confusion: Devotion to Mary Most Holy and frequent Communion."* Here we see that along with the Eucharist, Our Lady has been given to us as a Star on the stormy seas of earthly life to help guide us to safety one day in heaven.

Pope John Paul II also had beautiful things to say about Our Lady Star of the Sea:

> *"Stella Maris ('Star of the Sea') has long been the favorite title by which seafaring people have called on her in whose protection they have always trusted: the Blessed Virgin Mary. Jesus Christ, her Son, accompanied his disciples in their boat, helped them in their labors and calmed the storms. Thus the Church also accompanies seafarers, taking care of the specific spiritual needs of those who for various reasons live and work in the maritime world".* (From the Apostolic Letter Motu Propio 'On the Apostleship of the Sea', Pope John Paul II, 31 January 1997)

Virtues of Mary

Mary is considered our great Star –radiating the Light of Christ in crystal clear purity –because She was an abyss of virtue. Venerable Fr. Casimir Wyszynski, opened his own meditations on Mary's virtues with these words:

> *Mary is the noble Star rising from the house of Jacob, whose rays illuminate the whole world. ... Let us then watch the rise and movements of this brightest Star carefully; let us*

follow her; let us rise up from the sleep of death by sin. If we want to see this Morning Star rising, we must zealously imitate the ten Virtues of the Virgin Mary. For just as a star once led the three wise men to Jesus as he lay in a stable in Bethlehem, so will this Morning Star, shining with the ten rays of these evangelical virtues, lead us to Jesus sitting at the right hand of the Father in the heavenly kingdom.

Let us look very briefly at each of the 10 rays of this Morning Star, and see how Mary's example of virtue lights the way for us.

The first is <u>*purity*</u>.

Mary's second gospel virtue is <u>*prudence*</u>.

Mary's third gospel virtue is <u>*humility*</u>.

Mary's fourth virtue is <u>*faith*</u>: *this means the capacity to surrender oneself, in the heart and mind, to all that the Lord has revealed through Christ and His Church about His nature, His works, and His saving purposes for us. St. Elizabeth commended Mary for her faith with the words: "Blessed is she who believed that there would be a fulfillment of what was spoken to her from the Lord" (Lk 1:45). And Mary showed that she had surrendered herself completely to God, trusting Him to fulfill all His promises to Israel, when she declared at the end of her Magnificat (Lk 1:54-55):*

Mary's fifth evangelical virtue is <u>*devotion*</u>. *Of course, the English word "devotion" has several possible meanings, but here we use it to mean the virtue of using to the full all of the means of grace that our Lord has given to us to draw near to Him, especially prayer and the sacraments. Mary showed herself a truly devout woman of prayer when she offered, in praise and thanksgiving, her Magnificat, "My soul magnifies the Lord" (Lk 1:46), and again in the cenacle after Christ's ascension, when she was found at prayer in the midst of the disciples, waiting and praying for the special outpouring of the Holy Spirit promised by the Lord (Acts 1:14).*

We know that Mary was also given to prayerful meditation upon the mysteries of Christ, especially upon the wonders of His Nativity. Twice in the gospels we are told "she kept all these things, pondering them in her heart" (Lk 2:19, 51). The coming of the shepherds, the wise men, the star, and the prophecies: she treasured and cherished these memories, pondering them frequently, and uncovering their true meaning. This is an authentic exercise of religious devotion.

Mary's sixth virtue is obedience.
Mary's seventh evangelical virtue is poverty.
Mary's eighth gospel virtue is patience.
Mary's ninth gospel virtue is mercy or charity.

Mary's tenth evangelical virtue is sorrow. Of course, there is nothing especially virtuous just in "feeling sad." But whenever we take our pain, grief, and sorrow, and offer them up, in union with Christ's passion, then our sufferings can merit graces for the good of souls, both on earth and in purgatory. In this way, we can share in the redemptive work of our Savior (see Col 1:24). As Pope John Paul II taught in his apostolic letter on the meaning of human suffering, Salvifici Dolores: Our unavoidable sufferings and sorrows can find meaning in Christ, and can be put to good use. We are not only to do good to the suffering, he wrote, we are also to be good by our sufferings.

This is precisely what Mary did. As old Simeon had foretold, sorrow like a sharp sword would one day pierce her heart (Lk 2:35). She had a foretaste of this when she lost her 12-year-old son in Jerusalem at the time of the Passover, only to find him again in the Temple three days later (Lk 2:48). But Simeon's prophecy was fulfilled most of all at the time of the crucifixion of Jesus, as Mary remained faithfully with Him, standing at the foot of His cross, and bearing with Him the greatest sorrow that a mother's heart could ever endure: She witnessed the torturous death of an innocent man, her own beloved Son, the true Son of God.

Saint Louis de Montfort tells us that true devotion to our Lady is holy and it leads us to avoid sin and to imitate the virtues of Mary. The ten principal virtues that he focuses on in his writing are similar –they are: **deep humility, lively faith, blind obedience, unceasing prayer, constant self-denial, surpassing purity, ardent love, heroic patience, angelic kindness, and heavenly wisdom.** It is these virtues that make Our Lady brilliant with the Light of God

–a shining Star in our dark world (for She lived these virtues perfectly even while still in exile on earth) and a guide for us as we strive to imitate Her in order to reach heaven.

She is truly our Star. St. Faustina wrote in her beautiful prayer in *Diary* entry 1232:

O sweet Mother of God,
I model my life on You;
You are for me the bright dawn:
In you I lose myself enraptured.

O Mother, Immaculate Virgin,
In You the divine ray is reflected,
Midst storms, 'tis You who teach me to love the Lord,
O my shield and defense from the foe.

Saint Bonaventure noted that Our Lady, the Star of the Sea: *"guides to a landfall in heaven those who navigate the sea of this world in the ship of innocence or penance."* The Blessed Virgin Mary is a beacon and a lifesaver in our stormy seas. It is She of Whom the fourteenth chapter of the book of Wisdom speaks when it is written: *"You have established a steady path through the waves...But your providence, O Father! guides it, for you have furnished even in the sea a road, and through the waves a steady path, showing that you can save from any danger, so that even one without skill may embark..."* The Light of Divine Love in Our

Lady's Heart –coming from Her eyes, Her hands, Her presence –is the steady path we can follow in the midst of life's dangers to find a safe way back Home to heaven.

I already quoted the prayer that St. Bernard of Clairvaux wrote for Our Lady, Star of the Sea. But the Office of Readings for the Liturgy of the Hours for Feast of The Blessed Virgin, Mary Star of the Sea puts it in context of his longer homily:

(In praise of the Virgin Mary, Hom II, 17: SCh 390, PP168-170)

Depend upon the star, call upon Mary

Let us say a few words on this name, Stella Maris, which means star of the sea, and which is appropriately accorded to the Virgin Mother. Fittingly is she compared to the stars, since just as a star gives light without burning itself out, so the virgin gave birth to her son without stain to herself. As a star's light does not lessen its own brightness so neither does the Son lessen the Virgin's wholeness. She is therefore that noble star rising from Jacob which casts light over the whole world; whose splendor shines to the heavens and reaches down into the deep; which crosses the earth, warming spirits rather than bodies; fostering goodness and purging sins. And so I say that she is that bright and distinguished star to be raised above this vast ocean, sparkling with merit, shining with character. Whoever you may be, grasp that, as this age runs its course, you are tossed on the waves by gales and storms more than you walk upon dry land; do not turn your eyes from the beam of this star if you do not wish to be swamped by the storm! If the winds of temptation engulf you, if you are running onto the rocks of adversity, depend upon the star, call upon Mary. If you are thrown about on the waves of pride or ambition, speaking ill of others or jealousy, depend upon the star, call upon Mary. If anger or greed or the cares of the flesh batter your soul's boat, depend upon Mary. If you are unsettled by the hideousness of your sins, troubled by a bad conscience, terrified by the horror of the final judgment; if you are beginning to be dragged down into the pit of sadness, into the abyss of despair, reflect upon Mary. In danger; in distress, in doubt, reflect upon Mary, call upon Mary. Let her not leave your lips, let her not leave your heart and do not abandon your dealings with her if you wish to gain the object of your prayer.

Following her, you will not stray;
praying to her, you will not despair;
reflecting upon her, you will not go wrong.
With her taking your hand, you will not fall down;
with her protecting you, you will not fear;
with her leading you, you will not grow weary;
with her favor, you will accomplish;

and thus you will learn for yourself how truly it is said: And the Virgin's name was Mary.

But now, having pause for a moment, let us all who are passing through this life gaze upon the brightness of such a light. For in the words of the Apostle, It is good for us to be here, and it is pleasing to contemplate in silence what which many words fail to explain. In the meantime, while contemplating devotedly the shining star, the debate will be rekindled in what follows.

Response:

*R/. Virgin mother of Christ, you brought to birth the very likeness of God; shining star of the sea, watch over and protect us. *As you give birth and rejoice, the hosts of heaven sing praises.*

Reflections:

Infant, miracle of nature, *pray for us.*
Infant, prodigy of grace, *pray for us.*
Immaculate in thy Conception, *pray for us.*
Masterpiece of God's grace, *pray for us.*
Aurora of the Sun of Justice, *pray for us.*
Mirror of justice, *pray for us.*

Spiritual vessel, *pray for us.*

Vessel of honor, *pray for us.*

Singular vessel of devotion, *pray for us.*

Morning star, *pray for us.*

Cause of our joy, *pray for us.*

Beginning of our joy, *pray for us.*

End of our evils, *pray for us.*

Infant, joy of earth, *pray for us.*

Mary says, "As to My titles, I was the "Infant, miracle of nature" as I was the only place of God's creation not tainted by the stain of Adam and Eve's sin. Unsullied in My Immaculate Conception I was a 'prodigy of grace' –the 'Masterpiece of God's grace' –for the redemption My Son won for humanity was completed in totality within My being. For this reason Christ the Light shown fully and freely from within My soul upon the world, I was simply His Monstrance, an 'Aurora of the Son of Justice', a 'Mirror' of His Just and Merciful Love. I was the earthen vessel of the Son of God –a vessel of honor and a vessel of devotion –and His Light radiated from within My being to such a degree that everywhere I went '*His Light shone in the darkness and the darkness could not overcome it.*' (Jn 1:5) For this reason I bare the title 'Morning Star' –for I appeared in the darkness of humanity as a great promise of hope –the hope that My Son, the Savior, would soon herald in the New Day, the Eternal Morning of Heaven. His dawning upon this world is the cause of our joy, but this joy began to beat upon this earth when

He took flesh from My own Flesh –and in response to My Fiat became Incarnate within Me. He is the gift of the Father's eternal Joy to the world –and yet His Joy came forth from the Joy the Father experienced as He held My Immaculate Heart in His Fatherly Mind and Heart. My Jesus was from heaven and I was from earth –yet His Divine Redemption purified Me so fully that I along with Him was the joy of heaven and earth. This joy that comes forth from the fulfilment of the Father's original plan for humanity has power –it ends all evil –it quells all sin –it comforts all suffering and this Joy in Heaven heals and renews all of humanity. These are the great mysteries I reflected as My Son's Star of the Stormy Sea of this life. As He looked upon Me in contrast to the rest of fallen humanity, He was inspired with hope and joy as He pondered in My Heart the one creature Who together with Him always did His Father's will."

We Fly To Your Protection…

We fly to thy patronage, O holy Mother of God; despise not our petitions in our necessities, but deliver us always from all dangers, O glorious and blessed Virgin. Amen.

Loving Mother of the Redeemer

Loving Mother of the Redeemer, gate of heaven, star of the sea, assist your people who have fallen yet strive to rise again. To the wonderment of nature you bore your Creator, yet remained a virgin after as before. You who received Gabriel's joyful greeting, have pity on us poor sinners.

Ave Maria Stella

Hail, bright star of ocean, God's own Mother blest,
Ever sinless Virgin, Gate of heavenly rest.
Taking that sweet Ave, Which from Gabriel came,
Peace confirm within us, Changing Eva's name.
Break the captives' fetters, Light on blindness pour,
All our ills expelling, Every bliss implore.
Show thyself a Mother; May the Word Divine,
Born for us thy Infant, Hear our prayers through thine.
Virgin all excelling, Mildest of the mild,
Freed from guilt, preserve us, Pure and undefiled.
Keep our life all spotless, Make our way secure,
Till we find in Jesus, Joy forevermore.
Through the highest heaven, To the Almighty Three,
Father, Son and Spirit, One same glory be. Amen.

Prayer to Our Lady from St. Bernard of Clairvaux

If squalls of temptations arise, or thou fall upon the rocks of tribulation, look to the star, call upon Mary.

If thou art tossed by the waves of pride or ambition, detraction or envy, look to the star, call upon Mary.

If anger or avarice or the desires of the flesh dash against the ship of thy soul, turn thine eyes towards Mary.

If, trouble by the enormity of thy crimes, ashamed of thy guilty conscience, terrified by dread of the judgment, thou beginnest to sink into the gulf of sadness or the abyss of despair, think of Mary.

In dangers, in anguish, in doubt, think of Mary, call upon Mary.

Let her be ever on thy lips, ever in thy heart; and the better to obtain the help of her prayers, imitate the example of her life.

Following her, thou strayest not;
invoking her, thou despairest not;
thinking of her, thou wanderest not;
upheld by her, thou fallest not;
shielded by her, thou fearest not;
guided by her, thou growest not weary;
favored by her, thou reachest the goal.

And thus dost thou experience in thyself how good is that saying: 'And the Virgin's name was Mary.'

CHAPTER 5

Who is the Immaculate Mother
Our Seat of Wisdom – Our Lady of Fiat?

St Maximillian Kolbe in 'Will to Love' is quoted speaking of the Immaculate Conception and how Our Lady is God's Masterpiece:

"The Immaculata is the work of God and like every other such work is without comparison and entirely dependent upon her Creator. She is simultaneously the most perfect and most holy work of God for, as St. Bonaventure maintains: God can create a greater and more perfect world, but He

cannot exalt a creature to higher dignity than that to which he exalted Mary."

The Immaculata is the final 'line of demarcation' between God and creation. She is a faithful image of divine perfection and holiness.

The Immaculata never had the slightest trace of sin or stain of fault in her. Her love was always of the fullest, without the smallest imperfection. She loved God with her whole being, and love united her from the first moment of her existence in so perfect a manner to God that the angel at the Annunciation could say: 'Full of grace, the Lord is with thee.' She is, therefore, created of God, belonging to God, a reflection of God, an image of God, a child of God and the most perfect of human beings.

She is an instrumentality of God who with total awareness freely permits herself to be led by God and, in agreement with his will she desires to do only that which he commands, and acts in keeping with that will as perfectly as possible, without the smallest withdrawal of her will from the will of God. In the perfect use of the power and privileges entrusted to her, she fulfills always and in all things only and exclusively the will of God. This she does in love of God and in the Holy Trinity This love of God reaches such heights that it calls down the fruits of God's love.

At Lourdes our Lady, when questioned by Bernadette as to her identity, frequently replied: 'I am then Immaculate

Conception.' In these clear words she expressed the fact that not only was she immaculately conceived, but that she is the Immaculate Conception, just as something white differs from its whiteness, or something perfect from its perfection...

...That title contains many more mysteries which, with time, will be discovered. It points to the conclusion that, as it were, to the essence of the Immaculate pertains her Immaculate Conception. This title must be pleasing to her for it signifies her first grace, conferred upon her at the pristine moment of her existence, and the first gift is always the most beloved. This name is confirmed throughout her life for she was always immaculate and unsullied by sin. Whence, she is full of grace and God is ever with her; to that degree, moreover, that she became the Mother of the Son of God.

The Immaculata is in an ineffable manner united to the Holy Spirit as his Spouse, but in a manner incomparably more perfect than human words can express... On what does this dwelling of the Holy Spirit in the Virgin Mary depend? He himself is love in her, the love of the Father and the Son, a love by which God truly does love himself, the love of the whole Blessed Trinity, a fruitful love, a conception... the Holy Spirit lives in the Immaculata, in her soul, her being, and renders her fruitful from the very first moment of her existence and throughout her life and forever. This abeternal Immaculate Conception in the womb of her soul immediately initiates the divine life, her Immaculate Conception."

St. Louis de Montfort in 'True Devotion to Mary' says:

"Lord, you are always with Mary and Mary is always with you. She can never be without you because then she would cease to be what she is. She is so completely transformed into you by grace that she no longer lives, she no longer exists, because you alone, dear Jesus, live and reign in her more perfectly than in all the angels and saints...So intimately is she united to you that it would be easier to separate light from the sun, and heat from the fire. I go further, it would even be easier to separate all the angels and saints from you than Mary; for she loves you ardently, and glorifies you more perfectly than all your other creatures put together..."

St. Louis de Montfort's book 'The Secret of the Rosary' –the Chapter 'The Twentieth Rose':

"Are you in the miserable state of sin? Then call on the divine Mary and say to her: Ave, which means 'I salute thee with the most profound respect, thou who art without sin' and she will deliver you from the evil of your sins.

"Are you groping in the darkness of ignorance and error? Go to Mary and say to her: Hail Mary, which means "Hail thou who are bathed in the light of the Sun of Justice" –and she will give you some of her light.

Have you strayed from the path leading to Heaven? Then call on Mary, for her name means "Star of the Sea, the North Star which guides the ships of our souls during the voyage of this life,' and she will guide you to the harbor of eternal salvation.

Are you in sorrow? Turn to Mary, for her name means also 'Sea of Bitterness which has been filled with sharp pain in this world but which is now turned into a Sea of the Purest Joy in heaven,' and she will turn your sorrow to joy and your afflictions into consolation.

Have you lost the state of grace? Praise and honor the numberless graces with which God has filled the Blessed Virgin and say to her: Thou art full of grace and filled with all the gifts of the Holy Spirit, and she will give you some of these graces.

Are you all alone, having lost God's protection? Pray to Mary, and say: 'The Lord is with thee –and this union is far nobler and more intimate than that which He has with saints and the just –because thou art one with Him. He is thy Son and His Flesh is thy flesh; thou art united to the Lord because of thy perfect likeness to Him and by your mutual love –for thou art His Mother." And then say to her: "The Three Persons of the Godhead are with thee because thou art the temple of the Most Blessed Trinity," and she will place you once more under the protection and care of Almighty God.

Have you become an outcast and have you been accursed by God? Then say to Our Lady: "Blessed art thou above all women and above all nations, by thy purity and fertility; thou hast turned God's maledictions into blessings for us," and she will bless you.

Do you hunger for the bread of grace and the bread of life? Draw near to her who bore the Living Bread Which came down from heaven, and say to her: "Blessed be the fruit of thy womb Whom thou hast conceived without the slightest loss of thy virginity, Whom thou didst carry without discomfort and to Whom thou didst give birth without pain. Blessed be Jesus Who has redeemed our suffering world when we were in the bondage of sin, Who has healed the world of its sickness, Who has raised the dead to life, brought home the banished, restored sinners to a life of grace and Who has saved men from damnation." Without doubt, your soul will be filled with the bead of grace in this life and of eternal glory in the next. Amen."

Mirror of Justice –Mother Most Amiable

Because of Our Lady's exquisite holiness, She was a transparent Tabernacle –a Mirror –of the Holiness of Her Son. Her Immaculate Heart was full of the Wisdom of Her Son. And for this reason, She also bears the title 'Mirror of Justice.' Cardinal John Henry

Newman explained that the Marian title "Mirror of Justice" needs clarification to fully understand how Mary reflected Christ:

> *"Here first we must consider what is meant by justice, for the word as used by the Church has not that sense which it bears in ordinary English. By 'justice' is not meant the virtue of fairness, equity, uprightness in our dealings; but it is a word denoting all virtues at once, a perfect, virtuous state of soul—righteousness, or moral perfection; so that it answers very nearly to what is meant by sanctity."*

> *"Therefore when our Lady is called the 'Mirror of Justice,' it is meant to say that she is the Mirror of sanctity, holiness, supernatural goodness."*

> *"Do we ask how she came to reflect His Sanctity? —it was by living with Him. We see every day how like people get to each other who live with those they love ... Now, consider that Mary loved her Divine Son with an unutterable love; and consider too she had Him all to herself for thirty years. Do we not see that, as she was full of grace before she conceived Him in her womb, she must have had a vast incomprehensible sanctity when she had lived close to God for thirty years?"*

"We must recollect that there is a vast difference be-tween the state of a soul such as that of the Blessed Virgin, which has never sinned, and a soul, however holy, which has once had upon it Adam's sin; for, even after baptism and repentance, it suffers necessarily from the spiritual wounds which are the consequence of that sin. She never committed even a venial sin, and this special privilege is not known to belong to anyone but Mary."

The Marian title, "Mater Amabilis," today translated as "Mother most amiable," is also connected to Mary's sinlessness, Newman explained: *"Sin is something odious in its very nature, and grace is something bright, beautiful, attractive."*

"There was a divine music in all she said and did - in her mien, her air, her deportment, that charmed every true heart that came near her. Her innocence, her humility and modesty, her simplicity, sincerity, and truthfulness, her unselfishness, her unaffected interest in everyone who came to her, her purity - it was these qualities which made her so lovable."

Seat of Wisdom

Song of Songs 5:1 "I have come to my garden, my sister, my bride."

Our Lady's Heart is a Garden of Virtues from which the Son of God could take flesh and where the Christ Child could take rest. This is because the Holy Spirit was able to penetrate and possess Her body and soul in perfection from the very first moment of Her conception. This perfect Heart of the Child Mary is foreshadowed by the Book of Wisdom 7: 22-30 and 7:7-14:

"For in her is a spirit intelligent, holy, unique, manifold, subtle, agile, clear, unstained, certain, never harmful, loving the good, keen, unhampered, beneficent, kindly, firm, secure, tranquil, all-powerful, all-seeing, and pervading all spirits, though they be intelligent, pure and very subtle. For Wisdom is mobile beyond all motion, and she penetrates and pervades all things by reason of her purity. For she is a breath of the might of God and a pure emanation of the glory of the Almighty; therefore nothing defiled can enter into her. For she is the reflection of eternal light, the spotless mirror of the power of God, the image of his goodness. Although she is one, she can do all things, and she renews everything while herself purduring; Passing into holy souls from age to age, she produces friends of God and prophets. For God loves nothing so much as the one who dwells with Wisdom. For she is fairer than the sun and surpasses every constellation of the stars. Compared to light, she is found more radiant; though night supplants light, wickedness does not prevail over Wisdom."

"Therefore I prayed, and prudence was given me;

I pleaded and the spirit of Wisdom came to me.
I preferred her to scepter and throne
And deemed riches nothing in comparison with her,
nor did I liken any priceless gem to her;
Because all gold, in view of her, is a bit of sand,
and before her, silver is to be accounted mire.
Beyond health and beauty I loved her,
And I chose to have her rather than the light,
because her radiance never ceases.

Yet all good things together came to me with her,
and countless riches at her hands;
I rejoiced in them all, because Wisdom is their leader,
though I had not known that she is their mother.
Sincerely I learned about her, and ungrudgingly do I
    share—
her riches I do not hide away;
For she is an unfailing treasure;
those who gain this treasure win the friendship of God,
being commended by the gifts that come from her disci-
    pline."

This radiant Heart of Mary was chosen to be the Mother of God, and therefore the Mother of all Christians who make up the Body of Christ. If the Son of God was entrusted to Her care, nurturing and teaching, all the more we fallen sinners should look to Mary as

Our Mother, Instructress and Guide. In Sirach 15:2-8 and Sirach 51:13-21 we read:

She will meet him like a mother;
like a young bride she will receive him,
She will feed him with the bread of learning,
and give him the water of understanding to drink.
He will lean upon her and not fall;
he will trust in her and not be put to shame.
She will exalt him above his neighbors,
and in the assembly she will make him eloquent.
Joy and gladness he will find,
and an everlasting name he will inherit.
The worthless will not attain her,
and the haughty will not behold her.
She is far from the impious;
liars never think of her."

"When I was young and innocent, I sought wisdom.
She came to me in her beauty, and until the end I will cultivate
  her.
As the blossoms yielded to ripening grapes, the heart's joy, my
  feet kept to the level path because from earliest youth I was
  familiar with her.
In the short time I paid heed, I met with great instruction.

Since in this way I have profited, I will give my Teacher grateful
praise.
I resolved to tread her paths;
I have been jealous for the good and will not turn back.
I burned with desire for her, never relenting.
I became preoccupied with her, never weary of extolling her.
I spread out my hands to the heavens and I came to know her se-
crets.
For her I purified my hands; in cleanness I attained to her.
At first acquaintance with her, I gained understanding such that
I will never forsake her.
My whole being was stirred to seek her;
therefore I have made her my prize possession."

Mary as Virgin Mother

God's thoughts are above our thoughts and His ways are above our
ways. In order to best prepare a womb resplendent in perfection in
which to lay His Son, the Father determined to form not only an
Immaculate Heart that was to be called 'Mother', but also 'Virgin.'
In being completely consecrated to God and consumed by the Holy
Spirit as only a virginal heart can be, Our Lady was also made to be
the perfection of all Motherhood. Her Virginity was not a lacking
in something, but instead a gift of complete preservation so that
She could give Herself in totality to the King of kings. It was Mary's
Virginity offered to God in crystal clear fullness that enabled Him

to unite so perfectly with Her that She would be called not only the Mother of the Savior, but Mother of all of mankind. She would give birth to Jesus Christ the Head and then, beneath the Cross in union with Him, to His body the Church. Isaiah foreshadows this great mystery when it is written:

ISAIAH 54:1-8

Raise a glad cry, you barren one who never bore a child,
break forth in jubilant song, you who have never been in labor,
For more numerous are the children of the deserted wife
than the children of her who has a husband,
says the LORD.
Enlarge the space for your tent,
spread out your tent cloths unsparingly;
lengthen your ropes and make firm your pegs.
For you shall spread abroad to the right and left;
your descendants shall dispossess the nations
and shall people the deserted cities.
Do not fear, you shall not be put to shame;
do not be discouraged, you shall not be disgraced.
For the shame of your youth you shall forget,
the reproach of your widowhood no longer remember.
For your husband is your Maker;
the LORD of hosts is his name,
Your redeemer, the Holy One of Israel,
called God of all the earth.
The LORD calls you back,

like a wife forsaken and grieved in spirit,

A wife married in youth and then cast off,

says your God.

For a brief moment I abandoned you,

but with great tenderness I will take you back.

In an outburst of wrath, for a moment

I hid my face from you;

But with enduring love I take pity on you,

says the LORD, your redeemer.

ISAIAH 66:7-13

Before she is in labor,

she gives birth;

Before her pangs come upon her,

she delivers a male child.

Who ever heard of such a thing,

or who ever saw the like?

Can a land be brought forth in one day,

or a nation be born in a single moment?

Yet Zion was scarcely in labor

when she bore her children.

Shall I bring a mother to the point of birth,

and yet not let her child be born? says the LORD.

Or shall I who bring to birth

yet close her womb? says your God.

Rejoice with Jerusalem and be glad because of her,

all you who love her;

Rejoice with her in her joy,

all you who mourn over her—

So that you may nurse and be satisfied

from her consoling breast;

That you may drink with delight

at her abundant breasts!

For thus says the LORD:

I will spread prosperity over her like a river,

like an overflowing torrent,

the wealth of nations.

You shall nurse, carried in her arms,

cradled upon her knees;

As a mother comforts her child,

so I will comfort you;

in Jerusalem you shall find your comfort.

Rev 12:1-6

*"A great sign appeared in the sky, a woman clothed with
    the sun, with the moon under her feet, and on her
    head a crown of twelve stars.*

*She was with child and wailed aloud in pain as she la-
    bored to give birth.*

*Then another sign appeared in the sky; it was a huge red
    dragon, with seven heads and ten horns, and on its
    heads were seven diadems.*

*Its tail swept away a third of the stars in the sky and
hurled them down to the earth. Then the dragon
stood before the woman about to give birth, to devour
her child when she gave birth.*

*She gave birth to a son, a male child, destined to rule all
the nations with an iron rod. Her child was caught
up to God and his throne.*

*The woman herself fled into the desert where she had a
place prepared by God, that there she might be taken
care of for twelve hundred and sixty days."*

Reflections:

Holy Mother of God, *pray for us.*

Holy Virgin of virgins, *pray for us.*

Mother of Christ, *pray for us.*

Mother of the Church, *pray for us.*

Mother of Mercy, *pray for us.*

Mother of divine grace, *pray for us.*

Mother of Hope, *pray for us.*

Mother most pure, *pray for us.*

Mother most chaste, *pray for us.*

Mother inviolate, *pray for us.*

Mother undefiled, *pray for us.*

Mother most amiable, *pray for us.*

Mother admirable, *pray for us.*

Mother of good counsel, *pray for us.*
Mother of our Creator, *pray for us.*
Mother of our Savior, *pray for us.*
Virgin most prudent, *pray for us.*
Virgin most venerable, *pray for us.*
Virgin most renowned, *pray for us.*
Virgin most powerful, *pray for us.*
Virgin most merciful, *pray for us.*
Virgin most faithful, *pray for us.*
Seat of Wisdom, *pray for us.*

Mary says:

"In My Immaculate Heart was the fullness of God's grace. He was the source of My Virginity, My Motherhood and the fountain of Wisdom from within Me. Without being totally empty and pure, I could never have been engulfed by the absolute fullness of His Presence. In surrendering every atom of My Being as a Glass Tabernacle of His Abiding Love, He became incarnate within Me making Me at one time the Holy Mother of God, the Mother of Christ, the Mother of Our Creator, the Mother of Our Savior, the Mother of Divine Grace, the Mother of the Church and the Holy Virgin among all virgins. Under the Cross I also won the title of Mother of Mercy, Mother of Sinners, and Mother of Hope –as I offered perfect forgiveness in union with My Son to all of humanity and in perfect Compassion reached out with My Tears and

Prayer to help them step into repentance –to accept My Son's gift of Salvation. If I –the Mother of Jesus –could still love them after they killed My Child, then they had nothing to fear of the God of Love who created and sustained Me in this goodness. I was Mother most pure, Mother most chaste, Mother inviolate, Mother undefiled –and yet with the strength of the Holy Spirit I allowed the grave sins of humanity to be cast upon My Immaculate Heart as I offered Jesus' Love to everyone. It was the totality of My purity that allowed Me to be sustained so fully by Immaculate Love in the midst of such sin and filth –it was only because of My own lack of defilement that the Holy Spirit could fill Me with such powerful kindness to look with mercy upon sinners –in this I was the Virgin most Merciful. I was a Mother most amiable and a Mother most admirable because I was a selfless Mother before anything else –I accepted the fullness of God's Life within Me (to the point of Jesus being made incarnate within Me) –and I nurtured this Life and protected this Life and shared this Life with the world with every beat of My Heart and Breath of My lungs. The Holy Spirit Who is Wisdom Himself filled My Mind, Body and Heart so completely that I also am called the Mother of Good Counsel and Virgin Most Prudent –as I always listened attentively to His Will and followed Him in everything. In this I was His Virgin most faithful. I became His very Seat of Wisdom as Jesus –Wisdom Incarnate –took the place of His Throne within My Body, My Soul and upon My Motherly lap. I was the Virgin most venerable, Virgin most renowned and Virgin most powerful simply because of His majestic Divinity that united perfectly with My Humanity in the Incarnation. His power and glory shown out from Me –and yet My soul only magnified His Presence.

Learn from Me, My children, to be pure and surrendered as I am as your Virgin Mother. And know that to the degree you empty yourself to the grace and work of God is the degree My Son can come to live fully from within you. And know of My prayers for each one of you. Amen."

St. Louis De Montfort's Prayer to Mary

Hail Mary, beloved Daughter of the Eternal Father! Hail Mary, admirable Mother of the Son! Hail Mary, faithful spouse of the Holy Ghost! Hail Mary, my dear Mother, my loving Mistress, my powerful sovereign! Hail my joy, my glory, my heart and my soul! Thou art all mine by mercy, and I am all thine by justice. But I am not yet sufficiently thine. I now give myself wholly to thee without keeping anything back for myself or others. If thou still seest in me anything which does not belong to thee, I beseech thee to take it and to make thyself the absolute Mistress of all that is mine. Destroy in me all that may be displeasing to God, root it up and bring it to naught; place and cultivate in me everything that is pleasing to thee.

May the light of thy faith dispel the darkness of my mind; may thy profound humility take the place of my pride; may thy sublime contemplation check the distractions of my wandering imagination; may thy continuous sight of God fill my memory with His presence; may the burning love of thy heart inflame the lukewarmness of mine; may thy virtues take the place of my sins; may thy merits be my only adornment in the sight of God and make up for all that is wanting in me. Finally, dearly beloved Mother, grant, if it be possible, that I may have no other spirit but thine to know Jesus and His divine will; that I may have no other soul but thine to praise and glorify the Lord; that I may have no other heart but thine to love God with a love as pure and ardent as thine I do not ask thee for visions, revelations, sensible devotion or spiritual pleasures. It is thy privilege to see God clearly; it is thy privilege to enjoy heavenly bliss; it is thy privilege to triumph gloriously in Heaven at the right hand of thy Son and to hold absolute sway over angels, men and demons; it is thy privilege to dispose of all the gifts of God, just as thou willest.

Such is, O heavenly Mary, the "best part," which the Lord has given thee and which shall never be taken away from thee--and this thought fills my heart with joy. As for my part here below, I wish for no other than that which was thine: to believe sincerely without spiritual pleasures; to suffer joyfully without human consolation; to die continually to myself without respite; and to work zealously and unselfishly for thee until death as the humblest of thy servants. The only grace I beg thee to obtain for me is that every day and every moment of my life I may say: Amen, So be it--to all that thou didst do while on earth; Amen, so be it--to all that thou art now doing in Heaven; Amen, so be it--to all that thou art doing in my soul, so that thou alone mayest fully glorify Jesus in me for time and eternity. Amen.

CHAPTER 6
Who is the Sorrowful Co-Redemptrix?

O Weeping Mother, His Cross is in your eyes,
O Sad, Sad Savior, I find myself in Your glance, Your sigh
But now I've seemed to have lost my way, Your strength, Your peace.
Help me, Mother; O Savior, send Your grace.

Jesus, my Lover- as your spouse I need Your love.
O my Beloved- I beg Your Spirit, Your Fire, Your Peaceful Dove
My spirit weak- I need Your breath.
My body falls- I need Your step.

My mind is dark, Jesus, I need Your light.
I feel alone and blind, I need Your sight.
My heart is crying for Your touch, for Your kiss.
My soul lies in wait, I need renewal in Your midst.

O Weeping Mother, will you please pray for me?
O Broken Savior, please come set me free;
Wrap Your arms of love around me- hold me still.
How I want to trust in You as I mount Calvary's Hill.

O Good Jesus, take my heart so weak and small,
Do as you want with me, just please don't let me fall.
Place me on Your chest to sleep eternally.
O may Your Heart sing lullabies within me.

O Miriam, O Miriam, O Mother Come, pray for me.
Sweet Savior Come, rescue me.[2]

St. Maximillian Kolbe wrote:

---

[2] From song entitled 'O Weeping Mother' by Mary Kloska

"The Holy Spirit does not act except through the Immaculata, his spouse. Hence she is the Mediatrix of all the graces of the Holy Spirit. We may conclude that Mary, because she is the Mother of our Savior Jesus, became Coredemptrix of mankind, while by being the Spouse of the Spirit, she participates in the distribution of all graces."

"The cross, the manger, all the other mysteries in the life of Jesus are proof of his love for mankind. Who reflects upon it will repay that love with love.

One saint said that when house is afire, all within it is thrown out windows. So, too, the soul: when it is afire with the flame of divine love, it casts out all that is unnecessary, and concentrates all in the divine love.

Now, who loved the poor Lord Jesus in the manger and on the Cross more than His Blessed Mother? Neither angels nor human beings so love God as did the Mother of God. Let us not limit our love; let us love Jesus with her heart, for she loved him with that very heart. Let our love for God be the very love of the Immaculata. For this to be a reality, we must be hers; entirely, completely and in every way, hers."

Our Lady was not equal to Jesus –and yet She was created to be the 'New Eve', the 'Helpmate of Jesus the Eternal High Priest' in the work of His redemption. Fr. Paul Philippe and Hans Urs Von Balthasar explain this great mystery beautifully:

"St. Albert the Great says that the Blessed Virgin was not chosen by the Lord to be a minister, but to be a spouse and help, after the words of Genesis: 'Let us make for Him a helpmate like unto himself." (Gen 11:18) The Most Holy Virgin is not a Vicar, (that is to say an instrument), but a coadjutor and a **companion** *participating in the reign as She participated in the Passion... the wounds that Christ received in His Body, She felt in Her Heart.*[3]

"What then is the Role of Mary in the Passion? Nothing more than that of a help to Christ, 'a help like unto Himself' as St. Albert the Great says. For Mary is not formally a Priest on Calvary, but only the Associate of the Sovereign Priest. It is by Her union of charity with Christ that She collaborated in the Redemption, it is by Her Immaculate Heart that She is our Mother, as it is by His Sacred Heart that Jesus brought us into life.

Jesus told St Bridget, "Her Heart was in My Heart and that is why I can say that My Mother and I have saved mankind as with one Heart, I by suffering in My heart and My Flesh, and She by the sorrow of the heart and for love."[4]

His is a sacrifice that in the burning fire of suffering consumes within itself the entire godforsakenness of the sinner— and thus it is not only the cost physically but also the most

---

[3] Paul Phillippe, O.P., *The Blessed Virgin and the Priesthood* (Chicago: Henry Regnery Company, 1955), p. 36.

[4] [4] Phillippe, p. 61.

spiritually agonizing sacrifice of all. What, then, is Mary's position now in relation to this divine and human sacrifice?... **She embraces it with him, since She does not revoke Her Yes (fiat) but remains faithful to it to the last. She lets it be done. She offers to the Father, as She always has done, this self-sacrificing, sacrificial Victim, but in such a way that this offering (oblatio) is for Her the most heartrending renunciation, only thereby making Her oblation truly into a sacrifice, the surrender of what is dearest of all. How much sooner would the Mother suffer in the place of Her Son all that he has to undergo! How terrible it is to have to assent to this sacrifice, which, from a worldly perspective, is the most meaningless and hopeless of all!** *And when in Holy Mass, during the Canon, the Church again and again speaks of a sacrifice offered and recalls that it is not only the sacrifice of the Son that is commemorated but that the Church herself fully participates in the act of sacrifice, where else has She truly realized what this Her offering to the Father of the Son, costs Her except at that moment when, in Mary, She offered up Her Son to the Father? Sinners in the Church cannot in fact realize this; they must be glad, rather, that Christ offers himself for them. And the Church does not exist except in real subjects.* **Alone, this all-holy woman, and at most just a few others who have been purified to the point of purest love, can gauge what sword it is that pierces** *the heart of the Church when She for Her part sacrifices to the Father this self-sacrificing Lamb.*[5]

Mary Herself revealed this mystery to a mystic named Berthe Petit, who is much revered by the Church. She said:

"It is with a steadfast will that My Son wishes souls to have recourse to My Sorrowful Heart. I am awaiting this conversion in souls, My Heart overflowing with tenderness, asking nothing better than to pour into the Heart of My Son what is confided to My own, and to obtain graces of salvation for all."

Jesus said to Berthe as well:

"Teach souls to love the Heart of My Mother pierced by the very sorrows which pierced Mine...You must contemplate the Heart of My Mother, as you contemplate My own; live in that Heart as you wish to live in Mine; give yourself to that Heart as you give yourself to Mine; spread the love of Her Heart which is wholly united to Mine."

Our Lady often appeared to Berthe covered with the pain of Her Son's Passion. On one occasion She said: *"See here the wound*

---

[5] Hans Urs Von Balthasar, *Priestly Spirituality* (San Francisco: Ignatius Press, 2013), p. 49.

of My Heart similar to that of my Son, and the torrent of grace ready to gush forth from it..."

Later on Our Lady appeared again, her brow wounded and bleeding, her hands and Heart pierced. By those sacred stigmata, Mary showed how much She identified Herself with the sufferings of Jesus... and Mary said: **"You can now understand the sorrows which my Heart endured, the sufferings of my whole being for the salvation of the world."**

R. P. Garrigou-Lagrange, O.P. said:

"The grace of Her Immaculate Conception, together with the initial fullness of Charity, considerably heightened in Mary that capacity of Hers for suffering from the greatest of all evils which is sin. Souls suffer thus in the proportion of their love for God Whom sin offends, and of their love for souls whom mortal sin turns from their high destiny only to deserve eternal damnation. The Immaculate Heart of Mary was, therefore, Sorrowful in the very measure it was Immaculate and all-pure; in the measure with which the initial plenitude of Charity never ceased to grow in Her, until the moment of Her death.'

When we say 'Immaculate Heart of Mary' we recall that which She received at the moment of Her conception; when we say 'Sorrowful Heart' we recall all that she has suffered and offered for us, in union with Her Son –beginning with the words of the aged prophet Simeon up to the day She stood beneath the Cross on Calvary, and until Her own most holy death, shortly before Her Assumption."

Our Lady's Sorrows and Our Lady's Tears

It is by meditating on the holiness of tears (something often overlooked in our modern world) that we come to understand more deeply the power and beauty of Our Lady's Sorrows and Tears.

God loves and blesses tears. We see this in the book of Hezekiah when it is written, *"I have heard your tears..."* We see this when God reaches down in compassion from heaven to bless Hannah's prayer crying in the temple, Ester's prayer and tears, Joab's prayer and David's tears, as well as Job's tears. We see Jesus with Mary Magdalene when *"She washed His feet with her tears"* And JESUS DEFENDED HER. There is a great power in tearful prayers and love. We see this example best in Jesus' tears –at Lazarus' tomb where it is written *"And Jesus wept,"* in Gethsemane when He prayed *'With loud cries, prayers and supplications'* (Hebrews), on Calvary where it says that *'Jesus cried out with a loud voice.'* Jesus' tears were full of the power of Divine Love and Redemption -one tear of Jesus' could have saved the whole world.

Jesus always showed compassion on those who were crying. *How would Jesus have responded to His Mother's tears? -on Joseph's deathbed, for example? How would Jesus have responded to His little sister's tears? To a baby or child's tears? How did Jesus respond to* the wailing woman in the funeral procession? How did Jesus respond to Mary Magdalene's tears at Lazarus' tomb? How does Jesus respond to my tears? When Jesus saw people crying, He cried too. How did Jesus respond to the apostles crying out to Him during the storm at sea? How did Jesus (interiorly) respond to Peter crying after denying Him three times? (He looked 'with love'.) How did Jesus respond to the parents of the little girl who died before He raised her from the dead? How did Jesus' Heart respond to the crying of the Holy Innocents' slaughter ('Rachel's tears')? How did Jesus react to tears? What is God teaching us about tears?

"He stores my tears in His bottle and records them in His book."
–Ps 56:8

Jesus says:

"Tears are powerful. Tears of repentance, tears of sorrow, tears of joy –all tears are powerful –they are a way that the Lord washes the soul and gives a new perspective on one's life. Tears are a gift of the Holy Spirit –and when they are shed thus, they lead one's heart deeper into the Heart of Jesus and purify one's vision of His Reality of Truth and Reality of Love. It is a big mistake when people reject another's tears (or refuse to cry themselves), for tears are one of the deepest expressions of the human heart. I cried –at Lazarus' tomb, in Gethsemane, as a baby in Bethlehem, over Jerusalem, and on the Cross. So of-

ten the only language I spoke with My Father was that of crucified Love spoken through silence and a tearful pleading of the heart. I blessed other people's tears –the mother of the child of Nain who I met mourning her son and her tears moved me so fully that I raised her dead son back to life. I blessed the family's tears over their little girl and reassured them that their child was only sleeping. I blessed Mary Magdalene's tears crying over Me, crying in repentance, crying in love… I even publically defended her tears. I blessed Peter's tears after he denied Me three times, yes, I blessed his tears with the grace of true repentance as well as with the grace of knowing in his deep soul of My gift of forgiveness. Hannah's tearful prayer in the temple was blessed by a son, Samuel. Ester's and Suzanna's tears were blessed by the gift of My Father's deliverance. … it is powerful to meditate on My Heart's (and My Mother's) tears… Thank you for crying for Me, with Me, My child. I said that if people's hearts were hard and silent (with an ignoring silence of indifference) then I would make the rocks cry out. Your tears are better than a rock's tears (and think of how many statues I allow to cry to show people an icon of My presence and love.) All the more you should be that witness and proclamation of My Love by your tearful Love. Your tears add color to the world and they melt the Heart of the Father pleading for greater mercy for your heart and the hearts of your spiritual children."

"The people that escaped the sword have found favor
in the desert.
As Israel comes forward to be given his rest, the Lord
appears to him from afar:
With age-old love I have loved you;
So I have kept my mercy toward you.
Again I will restore you, and you shall be rebuilt, O
virgin Israel.
They departed in tears, but I will console them and
guide them;
I will lead them to brooks of water, on a level road, so
that none shall stumble.
For I am a Father to Israel, Ephraim is my first-
born." –Jeremiah 30

Even when there are tears, God offers hope. God doesn't only offer compassion or pity, but He offers a vision –a promise –of hope, of a resolution to the suffering.

"In Ramah is heard the sound of moaning, of bitter weeping!
Rachel mourns her children, she refuses to be consoled be-
cause her children are no more.
Thus says the Lord: **Cease your cries of mourning, wipe the**
tears from your eyes.
The sorrow you have shown shall have its reward, says the
Lord,

They shall return from the enemy's land.

There is hope for your future, says the Lord; Your sons shall
  return to their own borders.

...the Lord has created a new thing upon the earth:

***The woman must encompass the man with devotion."* –**
Jeremiah 31

Our Blessed Sorrowful Mother always united Her tears to that
of Jesus'. She invites us through Her Motherly Love to have the
courage to unite with Jesus' Passion as She did, to *'encompass 'the
Man' (Jesus) with devotion,'* remembering always that His resurrection from the dead has the last word. We see the Lord encouraging
His people in the midst of sorrow in the Old Testament already –
even before His Son came to redeem all death, sin and suffering.

"I am a man who knows affliction from the rod of his anger.

One who he has led and forced to walk in darkness, not in
  the light;

Against me alone he brings back his hand again and again
  all the day.

He has worn away my flesh and my skin, he has broken my
  bones;

He has beset me round about with poverty and weariness;

He has left me to dwell in the dark like those long dead.

He has hemmed me in with no escape and weighed me down
  with chains;

Even when I cry out for help, he stops my prayer;

He has blocked my ways with fitted stones, and turned my paths aside.

A lurking bear he has been to me, a lion in ambush!

He deranged my ways, set me astray, left me desolate.

He bent his bow, and set me up as the target for his arrow.

He pierces my sides with shafts from his quiver.

I have become a laughingstock for all nations, their taunt all the day long;

He has sated me with bitter food, made me drink my fill of wormwood.

He has broken my teeth with gravel, pressed my face in the dust;

My soul is deprived of peace, I have forgotten what happiness is;

I tell myself my future is lost, all that I hoped for from the Lord.

The thought of my homeless poverty is wormwood and gall;

Remembering it over and over leaves my soul downcast within me.

But I will call this to mind, as my reason to have hope:

The favors of the Lord are not exhausted, his mercies are not spent;

They are renewed each morning, so great is his faithfulness.

My portion is the Lord, says my soul, therefore will I hope
in him.

Good is the Lord to the one who waits for him, to the soul
that seeks him;

It is good to hope in silence for the saving help of the Lord.

It is good for a man to bear the yoke from his youth.

Let him sit alone and in silence, when it is laid upon him.

Let him put his mouth to the dust, there may yet be hope.

Let him offer his cheek to be struck, let him be filled with dis-
grace.

For the Lord's rejection does not last forever;

Tough he punishes, he takes pity, in the abundance of his
mercies;

He has no joy in afflicting or grieving the sons of men..." –
Lamentations 3:1-33

Not only Scripture promises us such hope, but the writings of
the saints do as well. St. Leo the Great wrote:

"Blessed are they who mourn, for they shall be com-
forted. But the mourning for which he promises eternal con-
solation, dearly beloved, has nothing to do with ordinary
worldly distress; for the tears which have their origin in the
sorrow common to all mankind do not make anyone blessed.
There is another cause for the sighs of the saints, another rea-
son for their blessed tears. Religious grief mourns for sin,

one's own or another's; it does not lament because of what happens as a result of God's justice, but because of what is done by human malice. Indeed, he who does wrong is more to be lamented than he who suffers it, for his wickedness plunges the sinner into punishment, whereas endurance can raise the just man to glory."[6]

Our Lady is honored not just because She suffered sorrow in itself, but **why** She suffered sorrow. She suffers in union with Jesus because of the sins of the world –yes, because they hurt Her Son, but also because they cast the souls committing them far from God Eternally. Her motherly, sorrowing Heart is reflected in Scripture:

"How long, O Lord? I cry for help but you do not listen!
I cry out to you, 'violence!' but you do not intervene.
Why do you let me see ruin? Why must I look at misery?
Destruction and violence are before me; there is strife, and
*   clamorous discord...*
...too pure are your eyes to look upon evil, and the
sight of misery you cannot endure..." –Habakkuk 1-2

"How lonely is she now, *the once crowded city!*
Widowed is she who was mistress over nations;

---

[6] St. Leo the Great -22nd Saturday in Ordinary Time, Office of Readings

The princess among the provinces has been made a toiling
slave.

Bitterly she weeps at night, tears upon her cheeks,
With not one to console her of all her dear ones;
Her friends have all betrayed her and become her enemies.
Judah has fled into exile from oppression and cruel slavery;
Yet where she lives among the nations she finds no place to
rest;
All her persecutors come upon her where she is narrowly con-
fined.
The roads to Zion mourn for lack of pilgrims going to her
feasts;
All her gateways are deserted, her priests groan, Her virgins
sigh;
She is in bitter grief.
...Come, all you who pass by the way, look and see whether
there is any suffering like my suffering..."
–Lamentations 1:1-4, 12

Following are examples from St. Isaac of Stella and St. Bernard of Clairvaux explaining beautifully the union of Christ's tears with that of the Church –of which Our Lady is the Prototype and Queen. Their sorrows are one, but because of this union, so is the efficacy of their prayer. St. Isaac of Stella wrote:

*"The prerogative of receiving the confession of sin and the power to forgive sin are two things that belong properly to God alone. We must confess our sins to him and look to him for forgiveness. Since only he has the power to forgive sins, it is to him that we must make our confession. **But when the Almighty, the Most High, wedded a bride who was weak and of low estate, He made that maid-servant a queen. He took her from her place behind Him, at His feet, and enthroned her at His side. She had been born from His side, and therefore He betrothed her to Himself. And as all that belongs to the Father belongs also to the Son because by nature they are one, so also the Bridegroom gave all He had to the bride and He shared in all that was hers. He made her one both with Himself and with the Father. Praying for His bride, the Son said to the Father: I want them to be one with us, even as you and I are one.***

And so the Bridegroom is one with the Father and one with the bride. Whatever He found in His bride alien to her own nature He took from her and nailed to His cross when He bore her sins and destroyed them on the tree. He received from her and clothed Himself in what was hers by nature and gave her what belonged to Him as God. He destroyed what was diabolical, took to Himself what was human, and conferred on her what was divine. So all that belonged to the bride was shared in by the Bridegroom,

and He who had done no wrong and on whose lips was found no deceit could say: Have pity on me, Lord, for I am weak. Thus, sharing as He did in the bride's weakness, the Bridegroom made His own her cries of distress, and gave His bride all that was His. Therefore, she too has the prerogative of receiving the confession of sin and the power to forgive sin, which is the reason for the command: *Go, show yourself to the priest.*

The Church is incapable of forgiving any sin without Christ, and Christ is unwilling to forgive any sin without the Church. The Church cannot forgive the sin of one who has not repented, who has not been touched by Christ; Christ will not forgive the sin of one who despises the Church. What God has joined together, man must not separate. This is a great mystery, but I understand it as referring to Christ and the Church.

Do not destroy the whole Christ by separating head from body, for Christ is not complete without the Church, nor is the Church complete without Christ. The whole and complete Christ is head and body. This is why he said: No one has ever ascended into heaven except the Son of Man whose home is in heaven. He is the only man who can forgive sin."[7]

---

[7] Office of Readings from the Friday of the 23rd Week of Ordinary Time –by Isaac of Stella

And from the holy abbot St. Bernard we have:

"The martyrdom of the Virgin is set forth both in the prophecy of Simeon and in the actual story of our Lord's passion. The holy old man said of the infant Jesus: He has been established as a sign which will be contradicted. He went on to say to Mary: And your own heart will be pierced by a sword.

Truly, O blessed Mother, a sword has pierced your heart. For only by passing through your heart could the sword enter the flesh of your Son. Indeed, after your Jesus—who belongs to everyone, but is especially yours— gave up His life, the cruel spear, which was not withheld from His lifeless body, tore open His side. Clearly it did not touch His soul and could not harm Him, but it did pierce your heart. For surely His soul was no longer there, but yours could not be torn away. Thus the violence of sorrow has cut through your heart, and we rightly call you more than martyr, since the effect of compassion in you has gone beyond the endurance of physical suffering.

Or were those words, Woman, behold your Son, not more than a word to you, truly piercing your heart, cutting through to the division between soul and spirit? What an exchange! John is given to you in place of Jesus, the servant in place of the Lord, the disciple in place of the master; the son of Zebedee replaces the Son of God, a mere man replaces God himself. How could these words not pierce your most loving heart, when the mere remembrance of them breaks ours, hearts of iron and stone though they are!

*Do not be surprised, brothers, that **Mary is said to be a martyr in spirit.** Let him be surprised who does not remember the words of Paul, that one of the greatest crimes of the Gentiles was that they were without love. That was far from the heart of Mary; let it be far from her servants.*

*Perhaps someone will say: "Had she not known before that he would not die?" Undoubtedly. "Did she not expect him to rise again at once?" Surely. "And still she grieved over her crucified Son?" Intensely. **Who are you and what is the source of your wisdom that you are more surprised at the compassion of Mary than at the passion of Mary's Son? For if He could die in body, could she not die with Him in spirit? He died in body through a love greater than anyone had known. She died in spirit through a love unlike any other since His."*[8]

---

[8] Office of Readings –Our Lady of Sorrows -From a sermon by Saint Bernard, abbot -His mother stood by the cross

The sorrows of this life are used by God to purify the faith, hope and love of souls that He draws to Himself. In the case of Our Lady who was already perfect, suffering expanded Her Heart to be a bigger Tabernacle of His grace and love for humanity. Once a soul undergoes suffering with Christ, their heart made single-hearted towards Christ's will united with the Father begins to pray with the efficacy of Jesus praying within him.

"Amen, amen, I say to you, you will weep and mourn, while the world rejoices; you will grieve, but your grief will become joy. When a woman is in labor, she is in anguish because her hour has arrived; but when she has given birth to a child, she no longer remembers the pain because of her joy that a child has been born into the world. So you also are now in anguish. But I will see you again, and your hearts will rejoice, and no one will take your joy away from you. On that day you will not question me about anything. Amen, amen, I say to you, whatever you ask the Father in my name he will give you." -John 16:20-23

Now we look at The Tears of Mary... they were in perfect union with the tears of Jesus –for their Hearts were always united as one and the tears of Jesus were physically composed from the body of His Mother.

When did Mary cry? What power do Her tears have?

Scientists have proven that the chemical make-up of tears is the same as sweat –with the purpose to get poison out of body caused by stress. When one works hard they sweat, and when one feels something profoundly, they cry. Tears are a great gift of communication –most often a communication of love. In Genesis we see man's punishment for sin was work and woman's was sorrow in childbirth. It is fitting that Christ, the New Adam, redeemed man with the sweaty work of the Cross in union with the consecrated tears of Our Lady, 'the New Eve', suffering as the Mother of the Church with Christ to give birth to Her from His pierced open Side.

Mary's Tears Under the Cross:

Mary's tears under the Cross were tears of frustration and anguish over others' sins and over others' cruelty… Her vision of truth was purer than others –and so She prayed with Jesus, *"Father, forgive them, they know not what they do…"*

Jesus said:

"My Mother's tears are golden –so pure that the Divine Light shines from them –because She cries them immersed alone in Her God in the garden of Her Heart – in the hermitage solitude of Her Love. There is nothing human in them –they are a pure refulgence of Divine Grace, a reflection of God's 'Sorrow' over man's sin –an incarnation of that sorrow, in a way, since God in Him-

self is pure Love and Joy. As the Will of God intersects with the fallen will of man, pain results to man and a disappointment of such touches God, although this is balanced in His Perfect adherence to justice and mercy. But for God to suffer with man, He had to become incarnate –and in order to cry with man, He needed incarnate tears.

My tears never contained anything of Myself within them –they were utter selfless Love over the sin and sorrow of man –or a reflection of the great joy in My Heart. As My Mother knew no sin, no separation of Her will from that of God's, Her Heart was always united perfectly with His Divine Life and Love –and this Life and Love filled Her tears as fully as it did My Own. As She prayed in the temple in the Holy of Holies as a small child[9], She would cry tears of praise, thanksgiving and joy for the fullness of God's presence both surrounding Her, as well as within Her. As She grew She cried in desire for His Love to be received fully by Her little human Heart, as well as for Him to be loved and adored in fullness here on earth as He was by the angels and patriarchs awaiting heaven. My Mother cried tears of sorrow and tears of joy each day of Her life as She watered Her prayer with this

---

[9] The Orthodox Church has the Tradition that Our Lady as a child in the Temple was allowed to pray in the Holy of Holies, because of the High Priest's prophetic sense concerning her purity and predilection (although exactly 'to what' was unknown, except for 'a great work of God.')

beautiful expression of Love. And yet these tears remained hidden from all, except for a few chosen souls – Joseph and John –called to witness Her Heart's Immaculate Love and to help Her carry the suffering weighing in Her Heart from being united to Mine.

My Mother cried tears of peace –of peaceful resignation to the holy will of Her Father in all things –a Fiat that gave forth life to all those the Holy Spirit tucked under Her surrendered abandon of Trust. Her tears of faith –especially in Her night of abandon on the Cross –gave birth to faith in the hearts of all souls entrusted to Her Motherly care and protection. You, too, live this mystery with Her. You nurse your children by your faithful fiat and suffering trust –a union of Love with Me, your Husband, and My Heart on the Cross and in the Eucharist. Yes, our Eucharistic, Crucified Love union purifies, enlightens, feeds and frees the world. The less they see, know and recognize this –the greater My power can work to transform the hearts around you –because of your hidden, humble, lowly, purified, totally selfless Love, which so reflects the Love of your and My Mother's Heart all the days of Her life –both on earth and in heaven.

Hers were tears of freedom –tears of 'Fiat' that won graces which freed others –those who are washed through Providence by Her grace..."

This teaching comes as seeds –a few ideas that Jesus buries in my heart that only later burst forth into flowers. One example is that of Mary's tears being 'stones'. *Many times have I felt that Jesus' tears would absolutely crush me –for each one He cried seemed to contain an eternity of sorrow and pain. When I see in my heart how Jesus is crying it is so heart-breaking, and as I offer Him my heart as His Kleenex to wipe His tears, or as His pillow that is soaked with His tears and blood as He lays upon it, these tears do seem heavy –and yet they pin me down close to Him and so it is a grace.*

Towards the end of my adoration I had a little vision in my heart of Our Lady crying over me, and Her Tears were brilliant as Gold –which I understood as a symbol of their purity and heavenly beauty. As they fell around me they were like stones that I saw crush the demons that were encircling me. When Jesus had told me weeks before that Mary's tears were 'like stones' I could not fathom what that could mean. But not only did I see them as huge golden stones around me, but I experienced their power as they literally crushed (and burned by their Golden, Fiery Love) satan and his minions surrounding and tormenting me. After Adoration I was able to attend another unexpected Mass and by the time I left my heart had total peace and clarity.

Luke 2:34: "Simeon blessed them and said to Mary his Mother, 'Behold, this child is destined for the fall and rise of many in Israel, and to be a sign that will be contradicted (and you yourself a sword will pierce) so that the thoughts of many hearts may be revealed."

The Orthodox have a beautiful icon entitled *'Tears before the Crucifix' Icon* – the image is of Our Lady surrounded by the causes of Mary's Tears, including:

-30 pieces of silver

-dice for His garments

-scourge/whip

-vinegar and gall

-4th cup chalice/ Eucharist

-hand that slapped Him

-nails, hammer, pliers

-thorns

-cock crowing

-darkness –red sun

-"INRI"

-tomb

-kiss of betrayal

-priest garments

-ropes

-sword

-outside the gates, the city

-the Cross' height

-Mary's own pure heart, love and suffering

Jesus said:

"Ocean of Love, Ocean of Tears, Ocean of Mercy. This is the fountain of Divine Life that I shared with My Mother's Heart from on top of Calvary. The putrid smell of sin and death suffocated us from all sides –yet deep within our 'two-made-one' Hearts of Fiat and Indwelling Love, purity was preserved and burst forth into the world even in the midst of exterior desecration and pain. The blood I shed on Calvary was My Mother's pure blood –since all of My humanity mysteriously came from Her. As were My tears of painful Love and Fiat with which I washed humanity actually Her tears (one with Mine both in their physical origin –My tears came from Her body –as well as in the source and purpose of their spiritual generation –our Hearts made one in suffering and prayerful surrender to My Father). And yet mysteriously on Calvary My Mother shed My tears –as they came forth from My pain within Her Heart. I received physical life from Her at the Annunciation when She prayed Her 'Yes' to My Father and opened both Her body and soul to receive His Spirit and Life Who created Me. But on Calvary it was She –the Mother of the Church, My Woman (Wife) Bride, who received life from Me. She, along with all of humanity was birthed forth anew from My side –from the blood and water, Spirit, Life and faithful Love pouring out from My wounded and ripped open Heart into the sacred chalice of Her Own. Her Heart was ripped open by the sword of Fiat –by Her Own prayer in union with My prayer to My Father in those moments. And in essence, this not only allowed Her to receive My Love and Life in a new way, recreating Her and all of humanity to be children of God (although Her actual reception of those graces of My Death on Calvary were given to Her earlier in time before Her conception), but it also filled Her as a wife is filled by her husband's life and love in a marital embrace. And through our union in pain, in surrender, in body and soul offered as a prayer of Love to our Father –She was able to help Me give birth to souls, to recreate My Life and Love in souls on earth, souls that would carry the image and reflection of our union of Trinitarian, Saving Love. Our Indwelling Love spoke through all the ages through the symbol of My blood and Her tears intermixing as one Eucharistic Sacrifice for the world.

Tears of joy, tears of pain, tears of innocence... that was the dowry My Mother gave to Me in our marriage on Calvary. And that is the dowry I desire for you to offer with Her...

"...The Tears of My Mother fell loudly as raindrops upon the parched land of dried up souls beneath My Feet on Calvary. Yes, My Mother's Tears were truly liquid –a sweet water to revive hardened hearts and to give them life by quenching their burning thirst. And yet, Her Tears also fell as balls of fire upon souls who had grown cold to the life of God and indifferent to My Pain. Her Tears were hurled forth as powerful cannon balls from Her Heart and exploded great graces to Her children gathered around Her on earth, yet also flowing forth throughout all time. For the source of these fiery tears was My timeless Love in Her Heart. These tears of fire warmed the cold earth –especially after My Death when all froze in silent emptiness at My Feet. These tears were candles, lamps to enflame the hearts wallowing in despair over their own sin, those content and comfortable in lethargic darkness, as well as those stuck in the mud of the oppressive war for their souls being raged by satan who tried to take advantage of God's visible absence from earth. Yet My Mother's tears truly crushed satan at that moment, although even he in his brilliant arrogance could not comprehend in totality how or why. He felt pinned still, immobile, at this seeming pinnacle of his victory –yet did not see it was the strength of My Mother's Tears, Her Love, that held him bound. My Mother's Tears were golden rocks that pinned him still. And these tears preserved the great echo of silence that rang through the earth –a silence that was necessary so that people could hear the sobbing of My Father's Heart in creation, as well as His *'It is Finished'* sigh of relief –His one, long breath of three days before His word *'Arise, My Beloved Son, and Come!'*

Those moments on Golgatha between the time I died and the time I was raised from the dead were moments that humanity is most especially indebted to My Mother Mary. This 'Woman of Sorrows' won more graces for humanity in those few hours and days then all of Her prayers and sacrifices of years before lived in union with Me. Her Heart alone held humanity in union with the Trinity through perfect faith, hope and love –a faith, hope and love perfected one with Me through the ultimate suffering of the Cross. In those moments of grief the joy She would one day live in heaven with Me was made full.

My Father walked with humanity in the Garden of Eden – carrying them in His Paternal Hand, under His Gaze. When they sinned and refused to let the light and love of His Divine Heart rest upon them, He continued to draw them little by little back to Himself through Me –the Incarnate Word –for all is seen from the Divine Perspective as an Eternal Present Moment. When My Sacrifice was complete and My Soul departed from My Body on the Cross, an earthquake shook the earth and the Veil in the Temple where He dwelt was torn in two. If My Father looked away from creation for a moment it would cease to exist –for His Love, His Gaze, His Attention gives it existence. Yet the Tear in His Divine Heart over the sins of His people reached such a climax at that moment it was as if He covered His Face in Sorrow and Shame –with their sorrow and shame contained within My Heart (both Human and Divine) –and this moment left the earth in utter empty darkness. The Holy Spirit of our Love remained present to sustain creation, yet for these moments He was immobile, held still in respect for My total gift of Love, held still waiting in and with humanity for My return, held still under the strain of upholding faith, hope and love in doubting, despairing and hateful hearts. Of course, all of these things I speak to you, My child, symbolically –for no human language can properly express the great, mysterious Truths I am feeding to your heart.

Yet in these moments after My death, awaiting My Resurrection –My Eucharistic Heart from the night of the Last Supper having been consumed –I did remain body and soul in one place on earth –and that was within the body and soul of My Mother. It is a scientific fact that cells and DNA from a child can be found within their mother's body up to 40 or 50 years after she gives birth to them. And yet all the more did I remain within the womb of My Mother's Heart –for our bodies were of the same substance, I came forth totally from Her physical make-up –the blood I shed *was Hers* –beating in My Heart that was a physical replica of Her Own. The Tears I shed on earth were Her Tears living in Me. And in a mysterious way My soul remained alive mystically incarnated within Her –as our Hearts and Souls were always knitted and seared together as one through our perfect union with the Trinity. There were aspects of My relationship with the Father that My Mother could not understand with Her human mind, since part of My relationship was Divine. Her humanity, for example, could not understand the concept of Our Eternal Union. Yet, My Mother's entire being was seeped in My Divinity, while being totally one with My Humanity –both through our union that was especially physical in the Incarnation, as well as our union of Love in the Spirit. And My Mother had received My Holy Presence in the Eucharist the night before I died –and She received Me in a way no human has ever been able to receive Me since –She received Me with an Immaculate Heart, and thus I was able to be totally, perfectly assimilated into Her –two made one –one Heart beating to glorify the Father, even in sacrifice.

Each Eucharistic Union of a soul with My Heart both as Human, and as God, reaches throughout one's entire life. Just as a beat of one's heart resounds throughout the entire body –so too one Eucharistic meeting with Me resounds throughout one's entire life –reaching outside of time back to its beginning and into its end and possible glorification with Me in heaven. Each Eucharistic Embrace you share with Me on earth purifies, strengthens, fills, transforms and changes not only you in the moment you receive –and not only thus your union with Me in the future –but also mysteriously touches, renews and transforms your human 'past' –it completely fills and consumes the totality of your 'life'. The depth that My touch and embrace can effect within you is dependent upon your freewill –your desire –your openness –your willingness to 'hug Me back' –your thirst to touch and be changed as one with Me. And in light of all this, My Mary, think of My Mother –who as My Eucharistic Gift pressed upon Her Lips and entered the chambers of Her Heart –lived the fullness of the effect of holiness My Being wanted to imprint within Her because of Her perfect Immaculate Heart, willingness, 'Yes –Fiat', combined with the greatness of My calling to Her to be My Mother. The single Eucharistic Embrace we shared the night before I died had already reached the depths of Her Body and Soul with My Presence –and having nothing foreign to God ever having existed within Her –this Presence remained full and transcending. And so somehow, mysteriously, I remained on earth even after My Death as My blood still raged within Her Veins, My Tears fell from Her Eyes, My very Spirit prayed from within Her and spurned Her along to *believe...* Yes, My Mother's perfect faith that night gave birth to My Presence in the world – and It was this faith –My Divine Faith living and beating in Her Soul –that gushed forth in Her tears thus crushing satan to the ground. The purity of Her Love in that moment gave birth to My Light in the world.

And so My Mother's Tears on Golgotha –Tears She shed in union with Me throughout all of My Passion –were tears of pure, liquid faith, hope and Love containing forgiveness and a plea for mercy that washed the sinful souls who killed Her precious Son. They were golden, like stone –crushing the power of hell raging to claim God's defeat –for even in the horror of decrepit darkness My Mother's Tears were a sign that She believed. They gave light in the night –although they poured forth so fully that they seemed to blind her, veiling Her vision of the body of Her Son. They spoke silence as the Great Silence of God's Fiat within them drowned out all noise on earth and beyond. And yet Her Tears on Golgotha were a song, a hymn of praise glorifying the Father with Her Love. Her Heart was wrung out in union with Mine. Her Tears exposed Her Heart in a way that is unfathomable for you to comprehend, My child. They spoke to the world of Her Vision of Heaven still alive in Her Heart, regardless of the hellish circumstances surrounding Her. They were a sign of the Presence of God in the midst of Her total abandonment. At that moment Her little Heart was an earthen vessel of the Divine –yet so intertwined was Her pain with My pain, Her fiat with My Fiat, that after My last breath emptied Her Heart, one could still not distinguish where My Love ended and Her Love began –for it was One Love –the Spirit's Love that we shared.

My Mother cried tears of frustration –the result of being tied to a humanity who so fully rejected God, yet allowing the nails of My suffering to stretch Her heart to offer them My Redemption. She truly is the Mediatrix of all My Grace. She cried tears of pain –human pain, for She was human – as well as spiritual divine pain over the rejection of salvation by so many. She cried tears of loneliness –but not even over Her Own loneliness. No, She cried tears over My suffering Loneliness that resulted from separation from My Father by taking the sins of mankind on Myself. She cried tears of repentance –as a good mother always will try to sacrifice to make up for and provide for her children –for all those who would refuse to cry their own. She cried tears of Fiat – just simple 'Fiat' surrender to the Father as an act of Her will in union with Me –in order to offer the just sacrifice of Her body and blood, heart and love hanging on the Cross in Her Jesus. She cried tears to glorify the Father... She cried the prayer I taught to your heart in adoration yesterday, My Mary –and you should always pray it in union with Her... *"Father, be glorified in Your Son Jesus, be glorified through the Holy Spirit, be glorified in me..."*

Tears come forth from the pain of one's life –and My Mother's Tears came forth from the pain of Her Son and God. One only suffers in heart to the degree he loves –and as My Mother's Heart was perfectly united with Mine, Her suffering was as infinite as My Love that dwelt within Her.

My Mother's Tears bore great fruit –for they were salt of love to flavor the tasteless, lukewarm hearts of Her children –they were light to penetrate their darkness –they were soap to wash their sin in union with Me –they were hope and strength to carry them on their journey towards heaven. So many mysteries are contained in My Mother's Tears... an infinite plenitude of mysteries...

As you began these weeks to meditate on Her tears, they have soaked into your heart and soul and begun to perfect it to be like Her Own. For your mystery to live on earth with Me is Her mystery of suffering Love on Calvary. My Mother's tears were pure – utter selflessness; they were humble –meek, lowly, human vessels to carry My Divine Love in Her Heart out to the world; they were powerful, because of their purity, humility and union with Me; they were holy –they were the prayer of perfect 'Fiat' to the Father, praising and thanking Him for such a great gift of Redemption and sharing in His depth of Love regardless of the pain. They were translucent –so clear, so light that My Heart's Blood and Presence could shine forth fully from within them. They were poor, docile, obedient, accepting the slavery of weakness and offering it to the Father in obedient trust. They created silence and called God to speak, and yet they themselves were His word –coming forth from Love they were a capsule of the Holy Spirit even in their anguish. And in some mysterious way, even on Calvary, My Mother's Tears contained joy –the joy that accompanies My Spirit and perfect, Fiat Love –for deep within My Mother was already rejoicing that Divine Love had conquered. She was so selfless on Calvary –crushed by humanity's cruelty and ugliness, yet all the while reaching forth with Her Motherly milk of co-redeeming Love to save them. They were the tears of a Mother. They were tears of a Wife who lives through marital love one with Her Husband's Being –even His pain. They were tears of a Bride –in innocence and hope. They were tears of a Widow –surrendering to death. They were tears of a Child, before Her Heavenly Father's Justice. They were tears of a Sister... of a Creature... of a little Flower beneath the Cross raised up to be a perfect mirror of Her Son's Love to the world. They were tears of peace, for they rested in the perfect will of My Father –

and this union soaked each molecule –in composition as well as in their union with Her Heart –with perfect peace. Yes, My Mother continued to help Me redeem even after My Death, by receiving My Fiat prayer into Her Heart, joining it through Her will in union with Her entire being, and praying it forth by Her Breath, Her Tears, Her Heart… and in this She lived a perfect Fiat with Me –and in this She cried peace into the hearts of humanity.

It is known that in suffering and stress, the human body creates poison that must be released through the cleansing of sweat and tears –formed by the same movements of one's heart and body. Suffering and stress entered humanity with Adam and Eve's first sin in Eden. Yet My Father immediately promised a remedy to this ugliness they chose –seeing My Heart's future gift of Calvary united with that of My Immaculate Mother's, He gave humanity the possibility to make up the justice due to God through union with My Redeeming Love. He did this by offering them the gift of sweat (*"By the sweat of your face shall you get bread to eat…" –Gen. 3:19*) and tears (*"In pain shall you bring forth children."*) –which united with the work of My Bloody Sweat of Calvary joined with the Sorrow of My and My Mother's Tears– made one in a perfect sacrifice of praise. Our work of redemption prayed 'Holy, Holy, Holy are You –O Lord, God of Hosts!' Yes, My Mother's 'Fiat' and sorrow completed My act of redemption –something which had to be received by humanity in order to be complete.

For the rest of your days She will live the mystery of Her tears in you.

"I have called you to live with Me a Eucharistic spirituality of the Cross with My Mother in union with My blood, My Wounds, My Love, My sacrifice, My Fiat and My Tears.

I am inviting you, My little, innocent, chosen one, My beloved one, into a love union with Me like that of My Mother. I created Her Immaculate so that when I, the Word, took flesh inside of Her womb and Her Heart, I would have an immaculately pure –translucent –little kingdom on earth from which to plant the Kingdom of My Father, and from which to reign. My Mother's 'Fiat' and subsequent conception of Me –the Eternal, Incarnate Word –made Her the Mother of God. ... As My Incarnation within My Mother's womb made Her to be the Mother of God – so will My mystical Incarnation within the womb of your heart, within the total gift of yourself to Me body, mind, heart, soul and spirit as My spouse –make you truly My little wife crucified. My Mother was always perfectly Immaculate –perfectly united to the Trinity in all thoughts, words, motives and deeds from the first moment of Her conception. Each breath of Her existence filled Her in a reciprocal indwelling of grace as She breathed in heaven, only to answer this gift by breathing it forth again. For this reason Her glory is of a magnitude unreachable by other human creatures.

And yet humanity is called to imitate Her in full –to perfectly become an icon of the Father's glorious Love and His Kingdom reigning in the Heart of His little creature spouse Mary –the maiden of Nazareth. My Mother's redemption was wrought for Her before Her conception –a free gift of My Love. Yet even if this predilection of grace was kept hidden from Her for a time,

She was always free to accept and multiply that grace by living 'Fiat' in union with My Father's will every moment of Her life. You were not born sinless like My Mother. My redemption of you has taken another form –one natural for those born into My Church after My death and resurrection. You were redeemed sacramentally –washed by the same merits of My Passion as My Mother was –but through an outpouring of grace in Baptism and stretching through the portals of My other Sacraments (Confession, Eucharist, Confirmation and Anointing of the Sick), as well as our union in prayer, in suffering and your concrete life of grace lived together with Me on earth. And yet I am no less intimately close to you than I was to My Mother when She was on earth –although being sinless from conception and exponentially growing in grace each moment of Her life, She was able to receive My Presence more deeply and fully into Her Heart and soul than you will ever conceive. And yet, the same fullness of the merits of My Passion is available to you. Those special graces of My Father's Love won by My Passion which ordained that She be Immaculately conceived, are poured out in their fullness within you from our _real_ Eucharistic –and yet all-encompassing –Sacramental Embrace.

I am Real –Body and Soul –within you as you receive My Eucharistic Heart. I beat the same heartbeat rhythm of Love that I do in Heaven and that I did on Calvary –the heartbeat that poured forth upon humanity the gift of Redemption –within the womb of your soul each time you meet with Me Sacramentally, especially in the Eucharist. I wash you with My real tears, blood, love, mercy and groans from the Cross as My entire Being intercedes for you from the Cross and draws you into My very Heart and Life each time you go to Confession, each time you've been Anointed, each time you open to Me in prayer allowing the fire of the Holy Spirit received in all these Sacraments -but especially in Confirmation -to rage within you in full. You were not immaculately conceived -but it is important for you to understand, My child, that <u>you have been immaculately redeemed</u>, <u>fully redeemed</u> -spotlessly redeemed, made anew, transformed to be a creature of My Father's Life and Light and glory as My Mother was -perhaps not similar in degree or merit, but equally full of Trinitarian Life and potential of fullness of union of one's being with the Trinity. The graces of such an <u>Immaculate Redemption</u> are available to you and all of humanity if you open your hearts and allow this grace to penetrate and transform you in full. In order to reach the heavenly shores of eternal life someday, you have to receive the gift of My redemption to your would perfectly in full. Comparisons are pointless in the Kingdom of Heaven -each soul is a different flower, a different story of My redeeming Love -yet each one holds the possibility of perfect and total union with Me -of reaching the perfection of self (through the merits of My Redemption) that was conceived by God for them from the beginning...

I want for you, My child, to receive the fullness of My Heart's redeeming Love within your soul tonight and always. I want you to allow Me to mystically live Incarnate within you as your Redeeming Husband and Lord. I want for you to pray your Fiat to My plan -My will for your life -with as much ardent trust as My Mother prayed that night in Nazareth at the moment of Her

Annunciation, as She lived in Bethlehem and Egypt, and as She lived on Calvary. I want you to rejoice in all the painful wounds of your life –even to the depths of your imperfections and sins, which you have offered to Me in the crucible of My Cross' pain – so that I can enter them, wash you with My very Self, Love and Presence within them as you are washed by 'The Word' made Flesh, join with you there and be made one with you within them –thus making you perfect and holy. *("Husbands, love your wives even as Christ loved the church and handed Himself over for her to sanctify her, cleansing her by the bath of water with the word, that He might present to Himself the church in splendor, without spot or wrinkle or any such thing, that she might be holy and without blemish." –Eph. 5:25-27)* And then I want to take you one step closer with Me as I ask you to join Me in My co-redeeming Love. As we began this teaching this afternoon, I want to end it here for now... My Mother, the Immaculate One, shared one Heart and body and soul with Me on Calvary. Her pain, united to My pain offered as one sacrifice to the Father opened torrents of grace for many souls. She was My truest Helpmate in redemption. And because of Her spotless union with Me, My deep moral suffering of taking mankind's sin onto Myself in order to redeem it –in order to make atonement for it to My Father through suffering the consequences of its pain and the 'separation from Him' it caused to My faculties all the while remaining united in a surrender of Love –was something My Mother suffered as a hideous death with Me. By far Her greatest sufferings were not over the physical pain or emotional loneliness or the relational betrayal of Her Son. Her greatest sufferings were My greatest sufferings –those of the moral, spiritual type –as She not only gazed at but shared with Her Son –the Sinless One –Who suffered the consequences of sin as if they were His Own –yet all the time in His will adhering only to the Father's Love, Will and Glory. This contradiction crucified My conscience and Heart –and this is the contradiction where satan entered as the accuser with all his fury, confusion, doubt, fear and despair trying to capture My vulnerability and trap My soul in imperfection. Yet even in this, My Heart and Soul cried out kindness and compassion *("Amen I say to you, today you will be with Me in Paradise." –Lk 23:43)*, cried out forgiveness *("Father, forgive them, they know not what they do." –Lk 23:34)*, cried out generosity and love *("Son, behold your Mother..." –Jn 19:27)*, cried out thirst and desire for My Father's Love *("I thirst." –Jn 19:28)*, cried out trustful prayer to Him in the midst of seeming abandonment *("My God, My God, Why have You abandoned Me?"-Mt 27:46; "Father, into Your Hands I comment My Spirit." –Lk 23:46)*, and cried out to accomplish His will to the end *("It is consummated... [finished]." –Jn 19:30)* This contradiction of willingly suffering for sin that I did not want nor agree to in action with My will as if it were My Own –a crucifixion of conscience in a way –I shared fully with My Mother as Co-Redemptrix, and this is the suffering I share with your heart as My little mystical wife, co-redeeming bride, as well.

"On that day you will realize that I am in my Father and you are in me and I in you." –Jn 14:20

"Whoever loves me will keep my word, and my Father will love him, and we will come to him and make our dwelling with him." –Jn 14:23

"Remain in Me, as I remain in you." –Jn 15:4

"I pray...so that they may all be one, as you, Father, are in me and I in you, that they also may be in us..." –Jn 17:21

"And I have given them the glory you gave me, so that they may be one, as we are one, I in them and you in me, that they may be brought to perfection as one... you loved them even as you loved me..." –Jn 17:22,23

"I made known to them your name and I will make it known, that the love with which you loved me may be in them and I in them." –Jn 17:26

There is a beautiful prayer called the *"Chaplet of Mary's Tears'* that is a powerful gift of grace. The prayers are a repetition of these prayers:

"O Jesus, behold the tears of the one who loved You most on earth and who loves You most ardently in heaven."

"Jesus, hear our prayers for the sake of the tears of Your most holy Mother..."

This prayer shows the efficacy of Our Lady's sorrows in interceding for us -each tear of Hers is a rose offered to God on our behalf –and so, a shower of Her tears is a shower of roses ascending to heaven to intercede for us. Mary's suffering and cries in order to water our souls and to soften our hardened hearts, lest one day it is said of us, 'they have no tears' just as in Cana she complained that 'they have no wine.' Tears are truly the wine of the Holy Spirit –a great gift from the Holy Spirit. The gift of tears is an actual charism of the Holy Spirit when a heart is united to Him. In this way, tears can be a prayer in themselves –as well as being a sign of one's complete 'Fiat' to God regardless of the cost.

Christ said that *'even the rocks will cry out!'* –and we see this gift of the Holy Spirit today in statues weeping. And yet, how much more precious to God is the miracle of a repentant heart weeping for their sins, or a heart so in love with their Savior that they cry over His Passion and Death.

So often the tears of Our Lady are misunderstood –seen through the prism of our own human experience of human tears which at times come from selfishness and make one's appearance age. Yet divine tears of Love renew a soul in youth, they purify and renew us (as rain renews the earth and its fruit). *How and over what do we cry? Do our tears reflect God's?* There are many types of tears –tears of repentance, tears of selfishness and greed, tears of joy, of pain, of self-pity, of surrender, of grace, of light and of peace –Our tears should renew us in Christ... if they do then they are an anointing of holiness and of beauty.

Our Lord Jesus Christ revealed to Blessed Veronica of Binasco, that He is more pleased in seeing His Mother compassionated than Himself. He said to her: **"*My daughter, the tears which you shed in compassion for My sufferings are pleasing to Me, but bear in mind*** *that on account of My infinite love for My Mother, the tears you shed in compassion for her sufferings are still more precious.*" Therefore the graces promised by Jesus to those who are devoted to the sorrows of Mary are very great.

St. Albert the Great said *"that as we are under great obligation to Jesus for His Passion endured for our love, so also are we under great obligation to Mary for the martyrdom which She voluntarily suffered for our salvation in the death of Her Son"*. He said 'voluntarily suffered' since it was revealed to St. Bridget by St. Agnes, *"our merciful and compassionate Mother was willing to endure any torment to save the souls of men."*

But She lamented to St. Bridget that very few did so, and that the greater part of the world lived in forgetfulness of them:

"I look around at all who are on earth, to see if by chance there are any who pity Me, and meditate on My Sorrows; and I find that there are very few. Therefore, My daughter, though I am forgotten by many, at least do you not forget me. Meditate on My Sorrows and share in My grief, as far as you can."

The Blessed Virgin told St. Matilda that when St. Simeon pronounced these words "all Her joy was changed into sorrow." For, as was revealed to St. Teresa, although the Blessed Mother already knew that the life of Her Son would be sacrificed for the salvation of the world, She then learned more distinctly and in greater detail what sufferings and what a cruel death awaited Him. She knew that He would be persecuted and opposed in every way.

Tower of Ivory

While an ivory tower is colloquially understood today as a privileged shelter from the practicalities of the real world, St. John Henry Newman connects Mary's title, "Tower of Ivory," to her courageous presence at the execution of her son.

> *"When we say a man 'towers' over his fellows, we mean to signify that they look small in comparison of him,"* he wrote. *"This quality of greatness is instanced in the Blessed Virgin. Though she suffered more keen and intimate anguish at our Lord's Passion and Crucifixion than any of the Apostles by reason of her being His Mother, yet consider how much more noble she was amid her deep distress than they were."*

> *"It is expressly noted of her that she stood by the Cross. She did not grovel in the dust, but stood upright to receive the blows, the stabs, which the long Passion of her Son inflicted upon her every moment... In this magnanimity and generosity in suffering she is, as compared with the Apostles, fitly imaged as a Tower."*

Reflections:

Health of the sick, *pray for us.*
Refuge of sinners, *pray for us.*
Solace of Migrants, *pray for us.*
Comfort of the afflicted, *pray for us.*
Help of Christians, *pray for us.*
Infant, health of the sick, *pray for us.*
Comfortess of the afflicted, *pray for us.*
Refuge of Sinners, *pray for us.*
Hope of Christians, *pray for us.*
Lady of the Angels, *pray for us.*
Daughter of the Patriarchs, *pray for us.*
Desire of the Prophets, *pray for us.*
Mistress of the Apostles, *pray for us.*
Strength of Martyrs, *pray for us.*
Glory of the Priesthood, *pray for us.*
Joy of Confessors, *pray for us.*

Mary said, **"My Son has already spoken to you at length about My sufferings and tears. His words are more than sufficient."**

Prayer composed by Berthe Petit during World War I. Promoted by His Eminence Cardinal Bourne and His Eminence Cardinal Mercier. Credited by the Cardinals for bringing an end to the war and granting numerous graces to mankind:

Prayer to the Sorrowful and Immaculate Heart of Mary

"O Lord Jesus, Who on Calvary and in the Holy Eucharist has shown Yourself to us as the God of Love and Mercy, kneeling humbly at Your feet we adore You and beg once more for Your forgiveness and Your divine pity. And remembering that by Your own act on Calvary, the human race, represented by Your beloved disciple John, gained a Mother in the Virgin of Sorrows, we desire to honor the sufferings and woes of our Mother's Heart by devoting ourselves to it in solemn Consecration. It is but just, O Mary, that our souls should strive henceforth to venerate you with special homage under the title of your Sorrowful Heart, a title won by sharing in the whole Passion of your Son and thus co-operating in the work of our redemption - a title due to thee in justice, and dear, we believe, to Jesus and to your own Heart, torn by the wound in His.

We consecrate therefore, O Mary, to your Sorrowful and Immaculate Heart ourselves, our families, our country and those who are fighting for its honor. Have pity on us; see our tribulations, and the anguish of our hearts in the midst of the mourning and calamities that lay waste the world. Deign, O Mother of God, to obtain mercy for us that, being converted and purified by sorrow, and made strong in faith, we may henceforth be devoted servants of Jesus Christ and His Church, for whose triumph we pray. O Mary Immaculate, we promise to be faithful clients of your Sorrowful Heart. Intercede for us, we beseech you, with your Son that, at the cry of your Sorrowful and Immaculate Heart, His Divine Power may speedily bring to pass the triumph of right and justice.

Sacred Heart of Jesus, have pity on us.

Sorrowful and Immaculate Heart of Mary, pray for us and save us."

Stabat Mater

At the cross her station keeping
stood the mournful Mother weeping,
close to Jesus to the last.

Through her heart, His sorrow sharing,
all His bitter anguish bearing
now at length the sword had passed.

Oh, how sad and sore distressed
was that Mother highly blessed,
of the sole-begotten One!

Christ above in torment hangs,
she beneath beholds the pangs
of her dying, glorious Son.

Is there one who would not weep,
whelmed in miseries so deep,
Christ's dear Mother to behold?

Can the human heart refrain
from partaking in her pain,
in that Mother's pain untold?

Bruised, derided, cursed, defiled,
she beheld her tender Child
all with bloody scourges rent.

For the sins of His own nation,
saw Him hang in desolation,
till His spirit forth He sent.

O sweet Mother! fount of love!
Touch my spirit from above,
make my heart with thine accord.

Make me feel as thou hast felt;
make my soul to glow and melt
with the love of Christ, my Lord.

Holy Mother! pierce me through,
in my heart each wound renew
of my Savior crucified.
Let me share with thee His pain,
who for all our sins was slain,
who for me in torments died.

Let me mingle tears with thee,
mourning Him who mourned for me,
all the days that I may live.
By the Cross with thee to stay,
there with thee to weep and pray,
is all I ask of thee to give.

Virgin of all virgins blest!,
Listen to my fond request:
let me share thy grief divine;

Let me, to my latest breath,
in my body bear the death
of that dying Son of thine.

Wounded with His every wound,
steep my soul till it hath swooned,
in His very Blood away;

Be to me, O Virgin, nigh,
lest in flames I burn and die,
in His awful Judgment Day.
Christ, when Thou shalt call me hence,
be Thy Mother my defense,
be Thy Cross my victory;

While my body here decays,
may my soul Thy goodness praise,
safe in paradise with Thee. ***Amen.***

CHAPTER 7

Who is our Queen?

Our Lady, Queen of our Hearts, Queen of Peace

"When she became Mother of the Creator, she truly became Queen of every creature." - Saint John Damascene

St. Maximillian Kolbe (as quoted in 'Will to Love') writes:

QUEEN OF HEAVEN AND EARTH *"In a loving family, the parents fulfill the desire of their children in all that is humanly possible, provided of course that what they ask be not harmful to them. All the more, Almighty God, the Creator and Model of earthly parents, desires to fully satisfy the will of his creatures, to the extent that what they will is not harmful to them, that is to the extent that it is in keeping with his will. The Immaculata never departed from anything that God's will demanded. In all things she loved the will of God, she loved God; hence she is rightly called 'The Omnipotent Beseecher,' and has influence with God over the whole of the universe, for she is its Queen in heaven and on earth. In heaven all recognize her say of love. And that portion of the angels who would not recognize her queenship, lost its place in heaven.*

She is also Queen of the earth, for she is the Mother of God. She desires and has a right to be freely recognized by every creature, by every heart, and to be loved as Queen of all hearts, so that through her, hearts would be cleansed and themselves become immaculate, similar and like unto her own heart, and so worthy of union with God, and with the divine love of the Sacred Heart of Jesus.

MOTHER, LADY, QUEEN

We call her Mother, but an earthly mother is not free of limitations, for even the law must sometimes protect children with respect to their parents. Meanwhile, she is a Mother without stain, immaculate indeed, and any reservation or restriction on the part of her children would rightly cause her ineffable pain and sadness.

We call her Our Lady, but that concept may draw us away from her maternal heart.

We call her Queen, but here, too we must be careful to add 'of all hearts,' Queen of Love. Her law is that of love, her power is maternal love."

Why is the Blessed Mother called a Queen? What other title would you give to the Mother of the Prince of Peace? A prince grows up to become a King. The mother of a King is given the title of Queen. Jesus is often referred to as our Lord and King of the Universe. And so Our Lady nobly deserves this title of Queen of Heaven and Earth. We celebrate Our Lady's Queenship in the Fifth Glorious Mystery: the Coronation of Mary as Queen of Heaven and Earth.

Pope Pius XII first established the Feast of the Queenship of Mary in 1954. But Mary's Queenship has its roots in Scripture. At the Annunciation, Gabriel announced that Mary's Son would receive the throne of David and rule forever. . In Luke 1:43 St. Elizabeth says, "*Who am I that __the mother of my LORD__ should come to me?*" By saying, '*__the mother of my Lord__*' Elizabeth is speaking of Our Lady in a royal way. Later on in Luke 1:48 as Our Lady prays the Magnificat, She Herself proclaims Her Queenship as She prays that "*all generations will call me blessed...*" The Blessed Mother's royalty is also evidently expressed by St. John in Revelation 12 (vs 1 and 5), where He writes about "*a woman clothed with the sun, with the moon under her feet, and on her head a crown of twelve stars... who gave birth to a son, a male child, destined to rule all the nations with an iron rod. Her child was caught up to God and his throne.*"

In the fourth century Saint Ephrem called Mary "Lady" and "Queen." Later Church fathers and doctors continued to use the title. Thomas à Kempis, author of the spiritual classic The Imitation of Christ once said, "What safer refuge can we ever find than the compassionate heart of Mary?" A well-known hymn calls the Blessed Mother "the Queen who decks her subjects with the light of God's own grace." As St. Antonius put it "Whoever asks and expects to obtain graces without the intercession of Mary endeavors to fly without wings."

The prayer "Hail Holy Queen," is a prayer of love to our mother Mary, composed in the 11th century, probably by a poor disfigured monk named Hermannus Contractus (d. 1054). This monk is sometimes referred to as Hermann the Lame, or Hermann the Cripple. He was born with a cleft palate, cerebral palsy and spina bifida; he had great difficulty moving and could hardly speak. When Hermann was 7 years old, his parents placed him in the care of the Benedictine monks of the abbey of Reichenau. Despite his physical disabilities, Hermann was a brilliant student and wrote several works on mathematics, astronomy, history and theology. Later in his life, his sight beginning to fail, Hermann is thought to have composed religious poetry and music, including the "Hail, Holy Queen."

> **Hail Holy Queen, Mother of mercy, Our life, our sweetness, and our hope. To thee do we cry, poor banished children of Eve. To thee do we send up our sighs, mourning and weeping in this valley of tears. Turn then, most gracious advocate, thine eyes of mercy toward us. And after this, our exile, show unto us the blessed fruit of thy womb, Jesus. O clement O loving O sweet Virgin Mary.**
>
> **V. Pray for us oh holy mother of God.**
> **R. That we may be made worthy of the promises of Christ.**

Mary has earned the title 'Queen of Heaven and Earth' in every way possible. Mary is "Queen by grace" because She was immaculately conceived, preserved from the slightest taint of sin while Her soul was literally inundated with divine grace. This is clearly evident in the Archangel Gabriel's greeting to Her: *"Hail, thou art full of grace."*

Mary is "Queen by divine relationship" for She is related in the first degree of consanguinity in the direct line to Our Lord and

Savior, Jesus Christ, the Son of God. A Queen Mother is one whose son later becomes king. Mary's Child, however at the moment of His birth, was already a King, the King of the world. Spiritual writers point out for our consolation that Mary's maternal relationship to Jesus was more exclusive than the other mothers, since He had no human father. Therefore, Our Lady was the Queen Mother from the first moments of Jesus' conception –and She was the 'Queen Mother' to a greater degree than any other mother on earth has ever been to her child –a future king.

Our Lady is Queen also "by right of conquest;" for She earned that title through Her faithful Fiat in perfectly fulfilling the will of the Heavenly Father in all things –even unto and beyond the death of Jesus on the Cross. Our Lord by His Passion and Death recaptured the human race from the slavery of Satan, conquering all as a King. Calvary was the scene of this conquest. During His Passion, Christ majestically said to Pilate, "My Kingdom is not of this world," so, too, Our Lady acknowledges herself in humility as a Queen whom all generations call blessed; but She, too, would add, "my kingdom is not of this world." Mary at the foot of the Cross shared intimately with Him in His Sacrifice and the fruits of the Redemption. And Mary's adherence to Her Son crucified, won for Her the title of 'Queen Mother of Mercy.' In the Litany of Our Lady, we address her as Queen of Angels, Patriarchs, Prophets, Martyrs, Confessors, Virgins; of Peace, of the Most Holy Rosary; Queen of Families, Queen conceived without original sin; and, Queen assumed into Heaven. Many prayers over the centuries have been written by saints and Popes, begging the powerful intercession of

Our Lady, Our Queen. And for centuries Christian art has represented the Blessed Mother as crowned with a diadem holding a scepter, seated on a throne –at the feet of Her Son.

As Our Lady is called the Mother of the Christ the King (which, in turn, makes Her Queen), She is also the Queen of His Body, the Church –which means that She is the Queen of all of us, Her faithful children. The Second Vatican Council explained: *"This maternity of Mary in the order of grace began with the consent which she gave in faith at the Annunciation and which she sustained without wavering beneath the cross, and lasts until the eternal fulfillment of all the elect. Taken up to heaven she did not lay aside this salvific duty, but by her constant intercession continued to bring us the gifts of eternal salvation. By her maternal charity, she cares for the brethren of her Son, who still journey on earth surrounded by dangers and cultics, until they are led into the happiness of their true home. Therefore the Blessed Virgin is invoked by the Church under the titles of Advocate, Auxiliatrix, Adjutrix, and Mediatrix. This, however, is to be so understood that it neither takes away from nor adds anything to the dignity and efficaciousness of Christ the one Mediator"* (Lumen Gentium, 62). Our Lady does not only advocate for us as a pious, holy person, but She advocates for us with the authority of the Queen Mother.

St. Alphonsus Ligouri explains this further in his book, ***The Glories of Mary:***

"The Church honors the Virgin Mary with the glorious title of Queen because She has been elevated to the dignity of Mother of the King of kings. If the Son is King, says Saint Athanasius, His Mother must necessarily be considered Queen. From the moment that Mary consented to become the Mother of the Eternal Word, She merited the title of Queen of the World and of all creatures. If the flesh of Mary, says Saint Arnold, was the flesh of Jesus, how can the Mother be separated from the Son in His Kingdom? It thus follows that the Regal Glory must not only be considered as common to the Mother and the Son, but must even be the same.

Mary, then, is Queen, but let all learn for their consolation that She is a mild and merciful Queen, desiring the good of all sinners. Therefore, the Church salutes Her in prayer and names Her the Queen of Mercy. The very name of Queen signifies, as Albert the Great remarks, compassion and provision for the poor; differing in this from the title of empress, which signifies severity and rigor. The greatness of kings and queens consists in comforting the wretched so that, whereas tyrants have only their own advantage in view, kings should be concerned with the good of their subjects. Therefore, at the consecration of kings, their heads are anointed with oil, which is the symbol of mercy, to denote that in ruling they should always show kindness and good-will toward their subjects.

Kings, then, should principally occupy themselves with works of mercy, but they should not neglect the exercise of justice toward the guilty when it is required. But Mary is not a queen of justice, intent on the punishment of the guilty, but rather a Queen of Mercy, intent only on compassion and pardon for sinners. Accordingly, the Church calls her Queen of Mercy. "These two things which I heard: that power belongs to God, and yours, O Lord, is kindness" (Psalm 62:12-13). The Lord has divided the kingdom of God into two parts, Justice and Mercy. He has reserved the kingdom of justice for Himself, and He has granted the kingdom of mercy to Mary. Saint Thomas confirms this when he says that the holy Virgin, when She consented to be the Mother of the Redeemer, obtained half (1⁄2) of the kingdom of God by becoming Queen of Mercy, while Jesus remained King of Justice...

...Is there anyone who does not know the power of Mary's prayers with God? Every prayer of Hers is like a law that mercy shall be given to those for whom She intercedes. Saint Bernard asks why the Church names Mary, Queen of Mercy. It is because we believe that She obtains the mercy of God for all who seek it, so that not even the greatest sinner is lost if Mary protects him.

But some might think that Mary hesitates in pleading on behalf of some sinners, because She finds them so sinful. Should the majesty and sanctity of this great Queen alarm us? No, says Saint Gregory, in proportion to Her greatness and holiness are Her clemency and mercy toward sinners who wish to repent, and have recourse to Her. Kings and queens inspire terror by the display of their majesty, and their subjects are afraid to go before them. But what fear, says Saint Bernard, can sinners have of going to this Queen of Mercy, since She never shows Herself austere to those who seek Her, but is always gentle and kind."

This gentleness and kindness of Our Lady, the 'Queen Mother of Mercy' are spoken of in **The Last Confidences** of St. Therese of the Child Jesus as well:

"Mary, then, is Queen, but Queen in the way of a Mother, serving all her children, guiding them in their most personal and intimate life, not so much by law and precept as by kindly prompting and persuasion, with an affectionate smile on Her countenance as She goes about bestowing a Mother's tender care on all Her children, on the lowliest no less than on the more fortunate. In fact, the more humble and lowly Her children, the more Mother She is to them. And the more we put ourselves in Mary's guiding care, the more quickly She leads us up to God.

In union with Christ, Mary guides the entire Church militant on the road to the City of God. But Mary's rule is marked, above all, by the supreme grace of Her Motherhood. She rules and directs souls with the power of a Mother's smile and the irresistible attraction of a Mother's sweetness. With a Mother's intuition She is ever alert, one might say, to yield to the supremely sovereign and kingly action of Her son, keeping Herself in the background, for even in Her own sovereign rule over the universe Mary is "more Mother than Queen."

Pope St. John Paul II spoke extensively in his General Audience on Wednesday, July 23, 1997 about the important role of Our Lady as our Queen, explaining how Her Queenship does not take priority over Her role as Mother, but instead ennobles it raising Her maternity to a greater glory. He said:

"Popular devotion invokes Mary as Queen. The Council, after recalling the Assumption of the Blessed Virgin in "'body and soul into heavenly glory'", explains that she was "exalted by the Lord as Queen over all things, that she might be the more fully conformed to her Son, the Lord of lords (cf. Rv 19:16) and conqueror of sin and death" (<u>Lumen gentium</u>*, n. 59).*

In fact, starting from the fifth century, almost in the same period in which the Council of Ephesus proclaims her "Mother of God", the title of Queen begins to be attributed to her. With this further recognition of her sublime dignity, the Christian people want to place her above all creatures, exalting her role and importance in the life of every person and of the whole world.

But already a fragment of a homily, attributed to Origen, contains this comment on the words Elizabeth spoke at the Visitation "It is I who should have come to visit you, because you are blessed above all women, you are the Mother of my Lord, you are my Lady" (Fragment, PG 13, 1902 D*). The text passes spontaneously from the expression "the Mother of my Lord" to the title, "my Lady", anticipating what St John Damascene was later to say, attributing to Mary the title of "Sovereign": "When she became Mother of the Creator, she truly became queen of all creatures"* (De fide orthodoxa, 4, 14, PG 94, 1157)

My venerable Predecessor Pius XII, in his Encyclical Ad coeli Reginam to which the text of the Constitution Lumen gentium refers, indicates as the basis for Mary's queenship in addition to her motherhood, her co-operation in the work of the Redemption. The Encyclical recalls the liturgical text: "There was St Mary, Queen of heaven and Sovereign of the world, sorrowing near the Cross of our Lord Jesus Christ" (AAS 46 [1954] 634). *It then establishes an analogy between Mary and Christ, which helps us understand the significance of the Blessed Virgin's royal status. Christ is King not only because he is Son of God, but also because he is the Redeemer; Mary is Queen not only because she is Mother of God, but also because, associated as the new Eve with the new Adam, she co-operated in the work of the redemption of the human race* (AAS 46 [1954] 635).

In Mark's Gospel, we read that on the day of the Ascension the Lord Jesus "was taken up into heaven, and sat down at the right hand of God" (16:19). In biblical language "to sit at the right hand of God" means sharing his sovereign power. Sitting "at the right hand of the Father", he establishes his kingdom, God's kingdom. Taken up into heaven, Mary is associated with the power of her Son and is dedicated to the extension of the Kingdom, sharing in the diffusion of divine grace in the world.

In looking at the analogy between Christ's Ascension and Mary's Assumption, we can conclude that Mary, in dependence on Christ, is the Queen who possesses and exercises over the universe a sovereignty granted to her by her Son.

The title of Queen does not of course replace that of Mother: her queenship remains a corollary of her particular maternal mission and simply expresses the power conferred on her to carry out that mission.

Citing Pius IX's Bull Ineffabilis Deus, the Supreme Pontiff highlights this maternal dimension of the Blessed Virgin's queenship: "Having a motherly affection for us and being concerned for our salvation, she extends her care to the whole human race. Appointed by the Lord as Queen of heaven and earth, raised above all the choirs of angels and the whole celestial hierarchy of saints, sitting at the right hand of her only Son, our Lord Jesus Christ, she obtains with great certainty what she asks with her motherly prayers; she obtains what she seeks and it cannot be denied her" (cf. AAS 46 [1954] 636-637).

Therefore Christians look with trust to Mary Queen and this not only does not diminish but indeed exalts their filial abandonment to her, who is mother in the order of grace.

Indeed, the concern Mary Queen has for mankind can be fully effective precisely by virtue of her glorious state which derives from the Assumption. St Germanus I of Constantinople, highlights this very well. He holds that this state guarantees Mary's intimate relationship with her Son and enables her to intercede in our favour. Addressing Mary he says: Christ wanted "to have, so to speak, the closeness of your lips and your heart; thus he assents to all the desires you express to him, when you suffer for your children, with his divine power he does all that you ask of him" (Hom. 1 PG 98, 348).

One can conclude that the Assumption favours Mary's full communion not only with Christ, but with each one of us: she is beside us, because her glorious state enables her to follow us in our daily earthly journey. As we read again in St Germanus: "You dwell spiritually with us and the greatness of your vigilance over us makes your communion of life with us stand out" (Hom. 1, PG 98, 344).

Thus far from creating distance between her and us, Mary's glorious state brings about a continuous and caring closeness. She knows everything that happens in our life and supports us with maternal love in life's trials.

Taken up into heavenly glory, Mary dedicates herself totally to the work of salvation in order to communicate to every living person the happiness granted to her. She is a Queen who gives all that she possesses, participating above all in the life and love of Christ."

Blessed Pope Pius XII wrote the following quotes concisely explaining the mystery of Our Lady's Queenship in His encyclical, <u>Ad Caeli Reginam</u> (On the Proclamation of the Queenship of Mary), promulgated on October 11, 1954:

"From the earliest ages of the catholic church a Christian people, whether in time of triumph or more especially in time of crisis, has addressed prayers of petition and hymns of praise and veneration to the Queen of Heaven. And never has that hope wavered which they placed in the Mother of the Divine King, Jesus Christ; nor has that faith ever failed by which we are taught that Mary, the Virgin Mother of God, reigns with a mother's solicitude over the entire world, just as she is crowned in heavenly blessedness with the glory of a Queen."

"In this matter We do not wish to propose a new truth to be believed by Christians, since the title and the arguments on which Mary's queenly dignity is based have already been clearly set forth...From early times Christians have believed, and not without reason, that she of whom was born the Son

of the Most High received privileges of grace above all other beings created by God...And when Christians reflected upon the intimate connection that obtains between a mother and a son, they readily acknowledged the supreme royal dignity of the Mother of God."

"The theologians of the Church, deriving their teaching from these [the Early Church Fathers] and almost innumerable other testimonies handed down long ago, have called the most Blessed Virgin the Queen of all creatures, the Queen of the world, and the Ruler of all...The Supreme Shepherds of the Church have considered it their duty to promote by eulogy and exhortation the devotion of the Christian people to the heavenly Mother and Queen."

"But the Blessed Virgin Mary should be called Queen, not only because of her Divine Motherhood, but also because God has willed her to have an exceptional role in the work of our eternal salvation. "What more joyful, what sweeter thought can we have" – as Our Predecessor of happy memory, Pius XI wrote – "than that Christ is our King not only by natural right, but also by an acquired right: that which He won by the redemption?..."

"Now, in the accomplishing of this work of redemption, the Blessed Virgin Mary was most closely associated with Christ; and so it is fitting to sing in the sacred liturgy: 'Near the cross of Our Lord Jesus Christ there stood, sorrowful, the Blessed Mary, Queen of Heaven and Queen of the World.'

Hence, as the devout disciple of St. Anselm (Eadmer, ed.) wrote in the Middle Ages: 'just as . . . God, by making all through His power, is Father and Lord of all, so the blessed Mary, by repairing all through her merits, is Mother and Queen of all; for God is the Lord of all things, because by His command He establishes each of them in its own nature, and Mary is the Queen of all things, because she restores each to its original dignity through the grace which she merited.'"

"Since we are convinced, after long and serious reflection, that great good will accrue to the Church if this solidly established truth shines forth more clearly to all, like a luminous lamp raised aloft, by Our Apostolic authority We decree and establish the feast of Mary's Queenship, which is to be celebrated every year in the whole world on the 31st of May [in the traditional calendar]. We likewise ordain that on the same day the consecration of the human race to the Immaculate Heart of the Blessed Virgin Mary be renewed, cherishing the hope that through such consecration a new era may begin, joyous in Christian peace and in the triumph of religion."

"In some countries of the world there are people who are unjustly persecuted for professing their Christian faith and who are deprived of their divine and human rights to freedom; up till now reasonable demands and repeated protests have availed nothing to remove these evils. May the powerful Queen of creation, whose radiant glance banishes storms and

tempests and brings back cloudless skies, look upon these her innocent and tormented children with eyes of mercy; may the Virgin, who is able to subdue violence beneath her foot, grant to them that they may soon enjoy the rightful freedom to practice their religion openly, so that, while serving the cause of the Gospel, they may also contribute to the strength and progress of nations by their harmonious cooperation, by the practice of extraordinary virtues which are a glowing example in the midst of bitter trials."

And here at the end of this chapter are five quotes of incredible saints proclaiming the greatness of Our Lady's role as our Queen Mother. May they be a compass pointing our way to Mary and inspire us with the courageous confidence we need to consecrate ourselves and every aspect of our lives to authority of Her Heart and Her prayers (and desires) for our lives.

"She has surpassed the riches of the virgins, the confessors, the martyrs, the apostles, the prophets, the patriarchs and the angels, for she herself is the first-fruit of the virgins, the mirror of confessors, the rose of martyrs, the ruler of apostles, the oracle of prophets, the daughter of patriarchs, the queen of angels." -St Bonaventure (1217-1274) Seraphic Doctor

"Mary has the authority over the angels and the blessed in heaven. As a reward for her great humility,

God gave her the power and mission of assigning to saints the thrones made vacant by the apostate angels who fell away through pride. Such is the will of the almighty God who exalts the humble, that the powers of heaven, earth and hell, willingly or unwillingly, must obey the commands of the humble Virgin Mary. For God has made her queen of heaven and earth, leader of his armies, keeper of his treasure, dispenser of his graces, mediatrix on behalf of men, destroyer of his enemies and faithful associate in his great works and triumphs." -St Louis Marie de Montfort

"To serve the Queen of Heaven is already to reign there and to live under her commands, is more than to govern." –St John Marie Vianney

"Prayer is powerful beyond limits when we turn to the Immaculata who is Queen even of God's heart." -St Maximilian Kolbe

"No one has access to the Almighty as His Mother has – none has merit such as Hers. Her Son will deny Her nothing that She asks and herein lies Her power. While She defends the Church, neither height nor depth, neither men nor evil spirits, neither great monarchs, nor craft of man, nor popular violence, can avail to harm us – for human life is short but Mary reigns above, a Queen forever." -St. Cardinal John Henry Newman

Reflections:

Our Lady, House of Gold, *pray for us.*

Tabernacle of the Christ child (visitation), *pray for us.*

Our Lady of the Rosary and Lapanto, *pray for us.*

Our Lady of Guadalupe, Fatima, Lourdes, *pray for us.*

Queen of Angels, *pray for us.*

Queen of Patriarchs, *pray for us.*

Queen of Prophets, *pray for us.*

Queen of Apostles, *pray for us.*

Queen of Martyrs, *pray for us.*

Queen of Confessors, *pray for us.*

Queen of Virgins, *pray for us.*

Queen of all Saints, *pray for us.*

Queen conceived without original sin, *pray for us.*

Queen assumed into heaven, *pray for us.*

Queen of the most holy Rosary, *pray for us.*

Queen of families, *pray for us.*

Queen of peace, *pray for us.*

Mary says, **"I am Queen. I am Queen of Heaven and Queen of Earth,1 Queen of bodies and Queen of all hearts. I am Queen of families, of relationships, of your work, vocation, ministry and life. I am Queen of your possessions and Queen of God's plans for your life. I am Queen –and I reign over all with My Son – because of My Love. To the degree a soul loves God and is cemented as one with Him through the Holy Spirit of Love is the** degree that one reigns with God in His Love. I have authority over heaven and earth because My Heart is Immaculate – absolutely nothing comes between any part of My being and that of God, His Love and His holy will for heaven and earth. Because of the authority that He entrusted to My Fiat and My Love, My prayer has efficacy before the throne of God unlike any other human who has existed or who will exist. My Heart glows as a furnace of Love for God, and so any intentions that you entrust to Me –even your very life that you entrust to Me –is thrown into this furnace of Love within Me, which is the Fire of the Holy Spirit –and purified and transformed and glows before God as an ember in the chamber of My Heart. For this reason, My prayers have an efficacy of Love unlike any other human being. My prayers for you have the efficacy of My Son's Love for you – crucified and risen."

CHAPTER 8
Consecration Prayer

Holy Infant Blessed Mother –my dearest Mama Maria Bambina –I come to You today as a poor, weak, empty, little sinner that I am. Before You I stand as Your weakest child –and yet dependent upon You for all things, I trust in the magnificence of Your powerful plan of love for my life. I, *(state your name)*, consecrate myself to You again this day –offering to Your purest arms, Heart and love –all who I am, all that I do, all who the Father desires me to become as a great saint in His eternal plan of love. I give You, my little Flower of Perfection Who always said Fiat to the Holy Spirit, my body, mind, heart, soul, spirit, emotions, memory, past, present, future, family, relationships, home, possessions, finances, work, ministry, desires, fears, hopes, and dreams and I ask you to weave them into the plan of Perfect Love that the Father keeps in His Heart for me. I give You, my littlest Mother, my complete Fiat, and I ask You to unite it with Your own as well as with Jesus' Fiat on the Cross, in the Resurrection and all of the days of His life. Make us one in our total trustful surrender to God's will in all things. Draw me into the womb of Your Immaculate and Sorrowful Heart, O Mother! Be my House of Gold, be the Star leading me to Your Son Jesus Christ, be the Mystic Rose whose perfume fills my entire being as I enter in to live within the center of Your Heart. O Holy Mother, be my Tower of Ivory- Whose faithfulness holds me firmly united as one to God in all things, especially to Jesus crucified.

Dearest Mother, my Lady of Czestochowa, Our little Mother of Guadalupe, Immaculate Mother of Sorrows, Prayerful Mother of Carmel, our Pilgrim Lady of Fatima, Lourdes, La Salette, Akita and

Kibeho, Our Lady the Never Fading Blossom, Our Mother clothed with the sun, my Hope of Perpetual Help, Good Remedy and Consolation, Our Lady, Undoer of Knots, my holy Queen of Peace, I ask for You to take my heart (name other's –the hearts of all of my family –both physical and spiritual) and the hearts of all those who Your Son desires to help me on the way of my vocation and I ask You to place them within the divine Light of the Holy Spirit's presence within Your Own Heart –and to give them to Jesus. Please ask Him to take our hearts and to pray over them each individually in a special way –remaking them, recreating and transforming them as He sees fit –to be identical to the hearts He desired for us to hold within our beings *from the beginning* –full of the Father's fresh breath of Love, Life, Humility, Holiness, Silence, Wisdom, Knowledge, Understanding, Patience, Courage, Temperance, Prudence, Fortitude, Kindness, Gentleness, Strength, Piety, Purity, Peace, Hope, Faith and Trust. Mary our Mother, I ask You to hold our hearts under the fountain of Love and Mercy that flows in Jesus' Blood and Water, Tears and Sweat, Fiat and Look, Forgiveness and Understanding, Hope and Trust –from each and every wound on His holy Body on the Cross, and most especially from His Heart. Just as His gift of redemption to us was concrete and physical in and through His body –I pray that it also touches and changes our minds, emotions, memory, psychology, spirit, soul and heart. May this redemption fall upon us through Jesus' breath – from on the Cross, in the Eucharist, and which You felt as He spoke to You resurrected. I ask that each of us is changed (healed, converted, enlightened and filled with perfect purity, wisdom, peace, surrender, courage, holiness, humility, silence and love) from this consecration to your Infant Immaculate and Sorrowful Heart, Jesus' Sacred Heart and Blood and to the Holy Spirit through your intercession.

No prayer asked through your intercession, my Mother, or through the power of Jesus' most holy wounds and in His Name will be ignored or denied by our Good Father in Heaven. And so please beg Jesus for me, my Mother, that He places His wounded Hands upon each of us –especially our hearts –and to pray for us to the Father and to heal, fill, convert, and transform us completely to be little images of you and the intimate love you share with Him. I ask Him, my Crucified Husband and Lord, to say the powerful words He so often said on earth when He prayed for those who asked His help: **'Be done, be healed, be delivered, be changed, be filled, be protected, be blessed –I want it, according to My Father's will!'** I ask to be one heart with Him, as a Siamese identical twin –united as Husband and wife in human and divine perfect Love. I especially ask for the seemingly impossible graces that burn in my heart and placed there by the Holy Spirit.

Mary, my little Infant Mother, I thank you for the example of humility, meekness and lowliness that you give to us in Your Holy Infancy –and I thank you for your beautiful, maternal and big sisterly Love. I re-consecrate my life and vocation to Your Most Perfect Heart, and to Jesus' most precious, wounded Heart on the Cross. I ask Him to fill my fiat (as He filled Yours) with His Father's Holy Will and His Spirit's powerful presence and to make all in my vocation, life, my family's lives, my spiritual children's lives be fulfilled perfectly according to His will. I give You everything, Jesus –through Mary. And I praise and thank You for Your perfect, never-ending, faithful Love. Please, set the fire of Your Love and Life in my vocation again –now and always. Help me trust in You! And help me receive ALL of Your Love! Jesus, have Mercy on us! Jesus, I trust in You! O Infant Sorrowful and Immaculate Heart of Mary, pray for us! Holy Mother, Maria Bambina, Queen of heaven and earth, pray for us!

CHAPTER 9
Preparatory Prayers and Extra Prayers

Consecration to Our Lady by St. Louis de Montfort

O Eternal and incarnate Wisdom! O sweetest and most adorable Jesus! True God and true man, only Son of the Eternal Father, and of Mary, always virgin! I adore Thee profoundly in the bosom and splendors of Thy Father during eternity; and I adore Thee also in the virginal bosom of Mary, Thy most worthy Mother, in the time of Thine incarnation.

I give Thee thanks for that Thou hast annihilated Thyself, taking the form of a slave in order to rescue me from the cruel slavery of the devil. I praise and glorify Thee for that Thou hast been pleased to submit Thyself to Mary, Thy holy Mother, in all things, in order to make me Thy faithful slave through her.

But, alas! Ungrateful and faithless as I have been, I have not kept the promises which I made so solemnly to Thee in my Baptism; I have not fulfilled my obligations; I do not deserve to be called Thy child, nor yet Thy slave; and as there is nothing in me which does not merit Thine anger and Thy repulse, I dare not come by myself before Thy most holy and august Majesty. It is on this account that I have recourse to the intercession of Thy most holy Mother, whom Thou hast given me for a mediatrix with Thee. It is through her that I hope to obtain of Thee contrition, the pardon of my sins, and the acquisition and preservation of wisdom.

Hail, then, O Immaculate Mary, living tabernacle of the Divinity, where the Eternal Wisdom willed to be hidden and to be adored by angels and by men! Hail, O Queen of Heaven and earth, to whose empire everything is subject which is under God. Hail, O sure refuge of sinners, whose mercy fails no one. Hear the desires which I have of the Divine Wisdom; and for that end receive the vows and offerings which in my lowliness I present to thee.

I, N_____, a faithless sinner, renew and ratify today in thy hands the vows of my Baptism; I renounce forever Satan, his pomps and works; and I give myself entirely to Jesus Christ, the Incarnate Wisdom, to carry my cross after Him all the days of my life, and to be more faithful to Him than I have ever been before. In the presence of all the heavenly court I choose thee this day for my Mother and Mistress. I deliver and consecrate to thee, as thy slave, my body and soul, my goods, both interior and exterior, and even the value of all my good actions, past, present and future; leaving to thee the entire and full right of disposing of me, and all that belongs to me, without exception, according to thy good pleasure, for the greater glory of God in time and in eternity.

Receive, O benignant Virgin, this little offering of my slavery, in honor of, and in union with, that subjection which the Eternal Wisdom deigned to have to thy maternity; in homage to the power which both of you have over this poor sinner, and in thanksgiving for the privileges with which the Holy Trinity has favored thee. I declare that I wish henceforth, as thy true slave, to seek thy honor and to obey thee in all things.

O admirable Mother, present me to thy dear Son as His eternal slave, so that as He has redeemed me by thee, by thee He may receive me! O Mother of mercy, grant me the grace to obtain the true Wisdom of God; and for that end receive me among those whom thou lovest and teachest, whom thou leadest, nourishest and protectest as thy children and thy slaves.

O faithful Virgin, make me in all things so perfect a disciple, imitator and slave of the Incarnate Wisdom, Jesus Christ thy Son, that I may attain, by thine intercession and by thine example, to the fullness of His age on earth and of His glory in Heaven. Amen.

Consecration to Mary by St. Maximillian Kolbe

O Immaculate, Queen of heaven and earth, Refuge of sinners and our most loving Mother, God has willed to entrust the entire order of mercy to You, I, an unworthy sinner, cast myself at Your feet, humbly imploring You to take me with all that I am and have, wholly to Yourself as Your possession and property. Please make of me, of all my powers of soul and body, of my whole life, death, and eternity, whatever pleases You. If it pleases You, use all that I am and have without reserve, wholly to accomplish what has been said of You: *"She will crush your head"*, and *"You alone have destroyed all heresies in the whole world."* Let me be a fit instrument in Your immaculate and most merciful hands for introducing and increasing Your glory to the maximum in all the many strayed and indifferent souls, and thus help extend as far as possible the blessed Kingdom of the Most Sacred Heart of Jesus. For, wherever You enter, You obtain the grace of conversion and sanctification, since it is through Your hands that all graces come to us from the Most Sacred Heart of Jesus.

V. Allow me to praise You, O most holy Virgin.

R. *Give me strength against Your enemies.*

St. Louis De Montfort's Prayer to Mary

Hail Mary, beloved Daughter of the Eternal Father! Hail Mary, admirable Mother of the Son! Hail Mary, faithful spouse of the Holy Ghost! Hail Mary, my dear Mother, my loving Mistress, my powerful sovereign! Hail my joy, my glory, my heart and my soul! Thou art all mine by mercy, and I am all thine by justice. But I am not yet sufficiently thine. I now give myself wholly to thee without keeping anything back for myself or others. If thou still seest in me anything which does not belong to thee, I beseech thee to take it and to make thyself the absolute Mistress of all that is mine. Destroy in me all that may be displeasing to God, root it up and bring it to naught; place and cultivate in me everything that is pleasing to thee.

May the light of thy faith dispel the darkness of my mind; may thy profound humility take the place of my pride; may thy sublime contemplation check the distractions of my wandering imagination; may thy continuous sight of God fill my memory with His presence; may the burning love of thy heart inflame the lukewarmness of mine; may thy virtues take the place of my sins; may thy merits be my only adornment in the sight of God and make up for all that is wanting in me. Finally, dearly beloved Mother, grant, if it be possible, that I may have no other spirit but thine to know Jesus and His divine will; that I may have no other soul but thine to praise and glorify the Lord; that I may have no other heart but thine to love God with a love as pure and ardent as thine I do not ask thee for visions, revelations, sensible devotion or spiritual pleasures. It is thy privilege to see God clearly; it is thy privilege to enjoy heavenly bliss; it is thy privilege to triumph gloriously in Heaven at the right hand of thy Son and to hold absolute sway over angels, men and demons; it is thy privilege to dispose of all the gifts of God, just as thou willest.

Such is, O heavenly Mary, the "best part," which the Lord has given thee and which shall never be taken away from thee--and this thought fills my heart with joy. As for my part here below, I wish for no other than that which was thine: to believe sincerely without spiritual pleasures; to suffer joyfully without human consolation; to die continually to myself without respite; and to work zealously and unselfishly for thee until death as the humblest of thy servants. The only grace I beg thee to obtain for me is that every day and every moment of my life I may say: Amen, So be it--to all that thou didst do while on earth; Amen, so be it--to all that thou art now doing in Heaven; Amen, so be it--to all that thou art doing in my soul, so that thou alone mayest fully glorify Jesus in me for time and eternity. Amen.

We Fly To Your Protection...

We fly to thy patronage, O holy Mother of God; despise not our petitions in our necessities, but deliver us always from all dangers, O glorious and blessed Virgin. Amen.

Loving Mother of the Redeemer

Loving Mother of the Redeemer, gate of heaven, star of the sea, assist your people who have fallen yet strive to rise again. To the wonderment of nature you bore your Creator, yet remained a virgin after as before. You who received Gabriel's joyful greeting, have pity on us poor sinners.

Ave Maria Stella

Hail, bright star of ocean, God's own Mother blest,
Ever sinless Virgin, Gate of heavenly rest.
Taking that sweet Ave, Which from Gabriel came,
Peace confirm within us, Changing Eva's name.

Break the captives' fetters, Light on blindness pour,

All our ills expelling, Every bliss implore.

Show thyself a Mother; May the Word Divine,

Born for us thy Infant, Hear our prayers through thine.

Virgin all excelling, Mildest of the mild,

Freed from guilt, preserve us, Pure and undefiled.

Keep our life all spotless, Make our way secure,

Till we find in Jesus, Joy forevermore.

Through the highest heaven, To the Almighty Three,

Father, Son and Spirit, One same glory be. Amen.

Litany of the Blessed Mother

Lord, have mercy on us. *Christ, have mercy on us.* Lord, have mercy on us.

Christ hear us. *Christ, graciously hear us.*

God, the Father of heaven, *Have mercy on us.*

God, the Son, Redeemer of the world: *Have mercy on us.*

God, the Holy Ghost, *Have mercy on us.*

Holy Trinity, One God, *Have mercy on us.*

Holy Mary, *pray for us.* (repeat at end of each phrase.)

Holy Mother of God,

Holy Virgin of virgins,

Mother of Christ,

Mother of the Church,

Mother of Mercy,

Mother of divine grace,

Mother of Hope,

Mother most pure,

Mother most chaste,

Mother inviolate,

Mother undefiled,

Mother most amiable,

Mother admirable,

Mother of good counsel,

Mother of our Creator,

Mother of our Savior,

Virgin most prudent,

Virgin most venerable,

Virgin most renowned,

Virgin most powerful,

Virgin most merciful,

Virgin most faithful,

Mirror of justice,

Seat of wisdom,

Cause of our joy,

Spiritual vessel,

Vessel of honor,

Singular vessel of devotion,

Mystical rose,

Tower of David,

Tower if ivory,

House of gold,

Ark of the covenant,

Gate of heaven,

Morning star,

Health of the sick,

Refuge of sinners,

Solace of Migrants,

Comfort of the afflicted,

Help of Christians,

Queen of Angels,

Queen of Patriarchs,

Queen of Prophets,

Queen of Apostles,

Queen of Martyrs,

Queen of Confessors,

Queen of Virgins,

Queen of all Saints,

Queen conceived without original sin,

Queen assumed into heaven,

Queen of the most holy Rosary,

Queen of families,

Queen of peace.

Lamb of God, who takest away the sins of the world, *Spare us, O Lord.*

Lamb of God, who takest away the sins of the world, *Graciously hear us O Lord.*

Lamb of God, who takest away the sins of the world, *Have mercy on us.*

V. Pray for us, O holy Mother of God.

R. *That we may be made worthy of the promises of Christ.*

Let us pray:

Grant, O Lord God, we beseech Thee, that we Thy servants may rejoice in continual health of mind and body; and, through the glorious intercession of Blessed Mary ever Virgin, may be freed from present sorrow, and enjoy eternal gladness. Through Christ our Lord. Amen.

Chaplet of Sorrows

Chaplet of Sorrows for Priests
1 Our Father

1 Hail Mary

1 Creed

On each 'Our Father' bead of a rosary, say the Sorrow of Our Lady's Heart and a Hail Mary.

On each 'Hail Mary' bead of a rosary, say:

"O Sorrowful and Immaculate Heart of Mary, Pray for us who have recourse to Thee!"

After all 7 decades, say 1 'Glory Be', 'Hail Holy Queen' and 'Memorare'

(You can also add the 'Sabet Mater' if you would like.)

Seven Sorrows of Our Lady (each one a 'Mystery' of the Chaplet)

1. <u>First Sorrow</u> of Our Lady's Heart is the Prophesy of Simeon

2. <u>Second Sorrow</u> of Our Lady's Heart is the Flight into Egypt

3. <u>Third Sorrow</u> of Our Lady's Heart is the Losing of the Child Jesus in the Temple

4. <u>Fourth Sorrow</u> of Our Lady's Heart is when Mary Meets Jesus on His Way to Calvary

5. <u>Fifth Sorrow</u> of Our Lady's Heart is when Jesus Dies on the Cross

6. <u>Sixth Sorrow</u> of Our Lady's Heart is when Jesus is Taken Down from the Cross and Laid in Her Arms (the 'Pieta')

7. <u>Seventh Sorrow</u> of Our Lady's Heart is when Jesus is Taken from Her Arms and Laid in the Tomb

<u>Chaplet of Our Lady's Tears</u>

(As given to Sister Amalia Aguirre (1901–1977) was a professed religious of the Missionaries of Jesus Crucified in Brazil.)

Beginning Prayer:

Crucified Jesus, prostrate at Your feet, we offer You the tears of the Mother who, with love full of devotion and sympathy, accompanied You on Your painful way to Calvary. Grant, O Good Master, that we take to heart the lessons which the tears of Your Most Holy Mother have taught us, so that we may fulfill Your Holy Will on earth and become worthy to praise and bless You in heaven for all eternity. Amen.

Large Beads *(instead of the "Our Father" say)*:

v. O Jesus, behold the tears of the One who loved You most while on earth,
r. And who loves You most ardently in heaven.

Small Beads *(instead of the "Hail Mary" say seven (or ten) times)*:

v. O Jesus hear our prayers,
r. For the sake of the tears of Your most holy Mother.

At the End *(repeat 3 times)*:

v. O Jesus, behold the tears of the One who loved You most while on earth,
r. And who loves You most ardently in heaven.

Concluding Prayer:

O Mary, Mother of Love, Mother of Sorrows and Mother of Mercy, we beg You, join Your prayers with ours so that Jesus, Your Divine Son to whom we turn, will graciously hear our petitions for the sake of Your maternal tears, and, together with the graces we implore, grant us finally the reward of eternal life. Amen.

With Your tears, O sorrowful Mother, destroy the dominion of Satan. Through Your divine tenderness, O bound and fettered Jesus, defend the world from the errors which threaten it. Amen.

Stabat Mater

At the cross her station keeping
stood the mournful Mother weeping,
close to Jesus to the last.

Through her heart, His sorrow sharing,
all His bitter anguish bearing
now at length the sword had passed.

Oh, how sad and sore distressed
was that Mother highly blessed,
of the sole-begotten One!

Christ above in torment hangs,
she beneath beholds the pangs
of her dying, glorious Son.

Is there one who would not weep,
whelmed in miseries so deep,
Christ's dear Mother to behold?

Can the human heart refrain
from partaking in her pain,
in that Mother's pain untold?

Bruised, derided, cursed, defiled,
she beheld her tender Child
all with bloody scourges rent.

For the sins of His own nation,
saw Him hang in desolation,
till His spirit forth He sent.

O sweet Mother! fount of love!
Touch my spirit from above,
make my heart with thine accord.

Make me feel as thou hast felt;
make my soul to glow and melt
with the love of Christ, my Lord.

Holy Mother! pierce me through,
in my heart each wound renew
of my Savior crucified.

Let me share with thee His pain,
who for all our sins was slain,
who for me in torments died.

Let me mingle tears with thee,
mourning Him who mourned for me,
all the days that I may live.
By the Cross with thee to stay,
there with thee to weep and pray,
is all I ask of thee to give.

Virgin of all virgins blest!,
Listen to my fond request:
let me share thy grief divine;

Let me, to my latest breath,
in my body bear the death
of that dying Son of thine.

Wounded with His every wound,
steep my soul till it hath swooned,
in His very Blood away;

Be to me, O Virgin, nigh,
lest in flames I burn and die,
in His awful Judgment Day.

Christ, when Thou shalt call me hence,
be Thy Mother my defense,
be Thy Cross my victory;

While my body here decays,
may my soul Thy goodness praise,
safe in paradise with Thee. ***Amen.***

Prayer to the Maria Bambina (Infant Mary)

Hail, Infant Mary, full of grace, the Lord is with thee, blessed art thou forever, and blessed are thy holy parents Joachim and Anne, of whom thou wast miraculously born. Mother of God, intercede for us.

We fly to thy patronage, holy and amiable Child Mary, despise not our prayers in our necessities, but deliver us from all dangers, glorious and blessed Virgin.

V. Pray for us, holy Child Mary.

R. *That we may be made worthy of the promises of Christ.*

Let us Pray: O almighty and merciful God, Who through the cooperation of the Holy Ghost, didst prepare the body and soul of the Immaculate Infant Mary that she might be the worthy Mother of Thy Son, and didst preserve her from all stain, grant that we who venerate with all our hearts her most holy childhood, may be freed, through her merits and intercession, from all uncleanness of mind and body, and be able to imitate her perfect humility, obedience and charity. Through Christ Our Lord. Amen.

Novena Prayer to the Maria Bambina (Infant Mary)

Holy Child Mary of the royal house of David, Queen of the
angels,
Mother of grace and love, I greet you with all my heart.
Obtain for me the grace to love the Lord faithfully during
all the days of my life. Obtain for me, too, a great devotion
to you, who are the first creature of God's love.
Hail Mary, full of grace................

O heavenly Child Mary, who like a pure dove was born
immaculate and beautiful, true prodigy of the wisdom of
God, my soul rejoices in you. Oh! Do help me to preserve
the angelic virtue of purity at the cost of any sacrifice.
Hail Mary, full of grace................

Hail, lovely and holy Child, spiritual garden of delight, where,
on the day of the Incarnation, the tree of life was planted,
assist me to avoid the poisonous fruit of vanity and pleasures of
the world.
Help me to engraft into my soul the thoughts, feelings,
and virtues of your divine Son.
Hail Mary, full of grace................

Hail, admirable Child Mary, Mystical Rose, closed garden,
open only to the heavenly Spouse. O Lily of paradise,

make me love the humble and hidden life;

let the heavenly Spouse find the gate of my heart always open

to the loving calls of His graces and inspiration.

Hail Mary, full of grace..............

Holy Child Mary, mystical dawn, gate of heaven,

you are my trust and hope.

O powerful advocate, from your cradle stretch out your hand,

support me on the path of life.

Make me serve God with ardor and

constancy until death and so reach an eternity with you.

Hail Mary, full of grace..............

Prayer:

Blessed Child Mary, destined to be the Mother of God and our loving Mother, by the heavenly graces you lavish upon us, mercifully listen to my supplications. In the needs which press upon me from every side and especially in my present tribulation, I place all my trust in you.

O holy Child, by the privileges granted to you alone and by the merits which you have acquired, show that the source of spiritual favors and the continuous benefits which you dispense are inexhaustible, because your power with the Heart of God is unlimited.

Deign through the immense profusion of graces with which the Most High has enriched you from the first moment of your Immaculate Conception, grant me, O Celestial Child, my petition, and I shall eternally praise the goodness of your Immaculate Heart.

IMPRIMATUR

In Curia Archiep. Mediolani

31 August 1931

Can. CAVEZZALI, Pro Vic. Gen

Litany in Honor of the Holy Infancy of The Blessed Virgin by St. John Eudes

Lord, have mercy on us,	*Lord, have mercy on us.*
Christ, have mercy on us,	*Christ, have mercy on us.*
Lord, have mercy on us,	*Lord, have mercy on us.*
Infant Jesus, hear us,	*Have mercy on us.*
Infant Jesus, graciously hear us,	*Have mercy on us.*
God the Father of heaven,	*Have mercy on us.*
God the Son, Redeemer of the World,	*Have mercy on us.*
God the Holy Ghost,	*Have mercy on us.*
Holy Infant Mary,	*Pray for us.*
Infant Daughter of the Father,	*Pray for us.*
Infant, Mother of the Son,	*Pray for us.*
Infant, Spouse of the Holy Ghost,	*Pray for us.*

Infant, fruit of the prayers of thy parents,	*Pray for us.*
Infant, Sanctuary of the Holy Trinity,	*Pray for us.*
Infant, riches of thy father,	*Pray for us.*
Infant, delight of thy mother,	*Pray for us.*
Infant, honor of thy father,	*Pray for us.*
Infant, honor of thy mother,	*Pray for us.*
Infant, miracle of nature,	*Pray for us.*
Infant, prodigy of grace,	*Pray for us.*
Immaculate in thy Conception,	*Pray for us.*
Most holy in thy Nativity,	*Pray for us.*
Most devout in thy Presentation,	*Pray for us.*
Masterpiece of God's grace,	*Pray for us.*
Aurora of the Sun of Justice,	*Pray for us.*
Beginning of our joy,	*Pray for us.*
End of our evils,	*Pray for us.*
Infant, joy of earth,	*Pray for us.*
Pattern of our charity,	*Pray for us.*
Model of our humility,	*Pray for us.*
Infant, most powerful,	*Pray for us.*
Infant, most mild,	*Pray for us.*
Infant, most pure,	*Pray for us.*
Infant, most obedient,	*Pray for us.*
Infant, most poor,	*Pray for us.*
Infant, most meek,	*Pray for us.*
Infant, most amiable,	*Pray for us.*
Infant, most admirable,	*Pray for us.*

Infant, incomparable,	*Pray for us.*
Infant, health of the sick,	*Pray for us.*
Comfortess of the afflicted,	*Pray for us.*
Refuge of Sinners,	*Pray for us.*
Hope of Christians,	*Pray for us.*
Lady of the Angels,	*Pray for us.*
Daughter of the Patriarchs,	*Pray for us.*
Desire of the Prophets,	*Pray for us.*
Mistress of the Apostles,	*Pray for us.*
Strength of Martyrs,	*Pray for us.*
Glory of the Priesthood,	*Pray for us.*
Joy of Confessors,	*Pray for us.*
Purity of Virgins,	*Pray for us.*
Queen of all Saints,	*Pray for us.*
Infant, our Mother,	*Pray for us.*
Infant, Queen of our hearts,	*Pray for us.*
Lamb of God, Who takest away the sins of the world,	*Spare us, Infant Jesus.*
Lamb of God, Who takest away the sins of the world,	*Graciously hear us, Infant Jesus.*
Lamb of God, Who takest away the sins of the world,	*Have mercy on us, Infant Jesus.*
Infant Jesus,	*Hear us.*
Infant Jesus,	*Graciously hear us.*

LET US PRAY

O almighty and merciful God, Who through the cooperation of the Holy Ghost, didst prepare the body and soul of the Immaculate Infant Mary that she might be the worthy Mother of Thy Son, and didst preserve her from all stain, grant that we who venerate with all our hearts her most holy childhood, may be freed, through her merits and intercession, from all uncleanness of mind and body, and be able to imitate her perfect humility, obedience and charity. Through Christ Our Lord. Amen.

The prayer of Saint Pope John Paul II to Our Lady Star of the Sea

MARY, STAR of the SEA, light of every ocean, guide seafarers across all dark and stormy seas that they may reach the haven of peace and light prepared in Him who calmed the sea. As we set forth upon the oceans of the world and cross the deserts of our time, show us, O Mary, the fruit of your womb, for without your Son we are lost. Pray that we will never fail on life's journey, that in heart and mind, word and deed, in days of turmoil and in days of calm, we will always look to Christ and say, 'Who is this that even wind and sea obey him?' Our Lady of Peace, pray for us! Bright Star of the Sea, guide us! Our Lady, Star of the Sea, pray for seafarers, pray for us.

CHAPTER 10
33-Day Preparation Schedule

After reading each day's reflections, it is suggested that the reader pray the Litany of the Infant Mary by St. John Eudes on pages 212-213. The reader is also encouraged to begin his or her consecration by praying St. Louis de Montfort's and St. Maximillian Kolbe's Consecration to Mary on pages 195-198. Finally, at the end of each day's reflections, the reader is encouraged to pray the prayers at the end of the chapter being read that day.

Day 1: Introduction -pages 1-4

Day 2: House of Gold -pages 5-6

Day 3: History of Maria Bambina Part 1 –pages 9-13

Day 4: History of Maria Bambina Part 2- St. Bridget -pages 13-19

Day 5: Devotion to the Maria Bambina Around the World –pages 19-24

Day 6: Who is the Maria Bambina –the Immaculate Virtue of the Infant Mary's Heart –pages 25-34

Day 7: The Name of Mary -pages 34-37

Day 8: First Reflections on the Litany of Mary –pages 37-41

Day 9: Who is the Mystical Rose? –pages 43-48

Day 10: The Holy Rosary –pages 49-51

Day 11: The Desert Rose –pages 51-56

Day 12: Second Reflections on the Litany of Mary –pages 56-60

Day 13: Who is the Morning Star –Star of the Sea? –pages 61-71

Mary Kloska's Vocation

For more information about Mary Kloska's vocation, books, icons (Artist Shop), music, podcasts, prayer ministry or to become a monthly donor to support her missionary work, please see:

www.marykloskafiat.com

Blog: http://fiatlove.blogspot.com

Books:

The Holiness of Womanhood:
https://enroutebooksandmedia.com/holinessofwomanhood/

Out of the Darkness:
https://enroutebooksandmedia.com/outofthedarkness/

In Our Lady's Shadow:
The Spirituality of Praying for Priests:
https://enroutebooksandmedia.com/shadow/

A Heart Frozen in the Wilderness:
Reflections of a Siberian Missionary:
https://enroutebooksandmedia.com/frozen/

Mornings With Mary: A Rosary Prayer Book:
https://enroutebooksandmedia.com/morningswithmary/

Raising Children of the Cross:
The Spiritual Formation of Children
Raising 'Children of the Cross' (the Spiritual Formation of Children) | En Route Books and Media

La Santidad de La Mujer:
https://enroutebooksandmedia.com/lasantidaddelamujer/

Swietosc Kobiecosci:
https://enroutebooksandmedia.com/swietosckobiecosci/

Z Ciemnosci:
Z ciemności… | En Route Books and Media

Fuera de las Tinieblas:
https://enroutebooksandmedia.com/fueradelastinieblas/

Radio Podcasts: https://wcatradio.com/heartoffiatcrucifiedlove/

YouTube VIDEO Podcasts
Playlist: http://www.tinyurl.com/marykloska

Artist Shop (Icon prints and other items for sale): http://marykloskafiat.threadless.com

<u>Music CD "FIAT"</u> is also available on all music platforms.

Please consider supporting Mary's Vocation and Ministry by becoming a monthly donor:
Patreon: <u>www.patreon.com/marykloskafiat</u>

OR

Please consider making a donation to the **<u>FIAT Foundation</u>** (a 501 (c) 3 tax-deductible foundation) to help in the printing and distribution of her books for free among the poorest of the poor –with a special emphasis on helping persecuted Christians throughout the world. Please contact Mary through her website (<u>www.marykloskafiat.com</u>) for more information about the FIAT Foundation.

To read about Mary Kloska's work specifically in Pakistan and Afghanistan, please see:
Memoir of Grace
written by her Pakistani Urdu translator Aqif Shahzad
<u>https://enroutebooksandmedia.com/memoirofgrace/</u>